ADVANCE PRAISE FOR
THE FIRST YEAR IS THE HARDEST

A satisfying fullness, like that from music, is contained in Jennifer Raphael's artwork, her six words for each week, and her honest narratives. She conveys the hard work of finding her heart, without shirking the growing complexity of her feelings and present actions. The mixed bag of her emotional past is explored for its secrets and epiphanies. By sharing the way she trained herself, she offers us insights into noticing "patterns that trigger resentment and feelings of inadequacy, stopping them before I feel shame, and redirecting the conversation toward a healthier outlook." (from week 15)

—Kenneth Buhr, PhD, Marriage and Family Therapist

In *The First Year Is the Hardest*, Jennifer Raphael uses her art to enhance the depth of each chapter. Raphael candidly expresses her feelings of resentment, loss, trepidation, and excitement and conveys those emotions in a way that reassures readers that they too will heal. I recommend this book to my clients who are transitioning from married to single life.

—Laurie Itkin, Financial Advisor and Certified Divorce Financial Analyst, author of *Every Woman Should Know Her Options*

Jennifer Raphael shares her struggle to rebuild a life and an identity in this layered and deeply personal account of starting over in the aftermath of divorce. The result is an affecting story of heartbreak, renewal and discovery. By courageously facing life and loss head-on, she learns to trust her own voice, allow space for the unbearable days and find healing and home inside her own skin.

—Cheri Reeder—friend, book lover, happy divorcée

This vulnerable exposé lays bare the real story of what it's like to navigate the emotional havoc of the first year of a marital breakup. Readers will find solace in realizing the "crazy" is both natural and surmountable through simple steps that will help them regain their lives. Highly recommended!

—Melody A. Kramer, Founder Legal Greenhouse and author,
Why Lawyers Suck! Hacking The Legal System, Part One

THE FIRST YEAR
IS THE HARDEST

Grief-Pain-Loss: Dissolution of Marriage

Healing Six Words At A Time

JENNIFER L. RAPHAEL

Printed and bound in the United States of America
ISBN: 978-0-692-94340-3

Photography and interior illustrations by Jennifer L. Raphael
Cover illustration by Brenna Seines

To Brenna and Trevor. I could not love you more.

PREFACE

I am a single, 59-year-old woman with two adult children. I was married for 25 years. I was faithful. I was devoted to my husband and children. I worked hard to make our daily life beautiful and safe and happy.

It wasn't enough. And my heart broke.

For something as commonplace as heartbreak, it seems that there should be an established formula for recovery. But there isn't. The closest thing that I have found to a cure came from embracing the following six words: "The first year is the hardest."

Those six words inspired this book. Those six words inspired me and gave me hope and courage. And I wondered, if I could embrace recovery from this loss and get through my grief by clinging to these six words, could sharing those same words help others?

And so it began. I looked for six words to describe what I was feeling, where I struggled, what I questioned, and what inspired me so that I could turn around at the end of it all and offer my hand to someone else struggling with the loss and grief surrounding divorce.

I was a train wreck. But I had survived setbacks in my life before. I knew deep down inside that I could do it again. And I hoped that sharing my story would lessen someone else's pain along the way.

What I have learned is this: "The first year," the one that *they* say is the most difficult, is a metaphor for allowing time and space to put your thoughts into perspective, to learn who you are on your own, and to find your "new normal."

Hearing this, hoping it was true, and then believing it were the first steps toward healing my broken heart and my broken spirit.

My "first year" started the day I discovered the depth of the deception, lies, and betrayal.

There had been sorrow and difficulty leading up to that day, as in any marriage. If I am being honest, there had been days and even months when I wondered if I was fighting a losing battle to save our relationship and to save my husband from his moods and insecurities. But always, I asked myself to be strong, to be hopeful, and to focus on the blessings in every day. After all, there was much to appreciate, and things could be worse.

And I was right about that. Things could become worse, and they did.

I was packing and preparing for our family vacation, doing all the things that I always do to leave home so that I can truly enjoy time away with my family. As the part-time stay-at-home mom, part-time business owner, and extraordinary residential organizer by nature, all the details of planning and organizing anything and everything in our family unrelated to my husband's job were my domain. And this included a quick look at a few things on my computer to learn what last details needed my attention. We were to leave for Catalina Island two days later.

What I saw were my husband's private emails, open for me to read. And, yes, I could have closed the email server right then and there and looked away. But I didn't.

And what I read made it difficult to breathe. Personal, private conversations with the woman I came to think of as "The Black Widow" were there in a folder marked VIP. His flirtations and assignations with her were there in black and white.

Had he left this for me to see? Was leaving the evidence easier for him than telling me face to face? I could no longer make excuses for his long absences, his inattention to me, his disconnection from family. I felt confused, betrayed, and so very hurt. Despite my discovery of this secret life, he wanted to take the planned family vacation as if nothing had changed, *"for our children's sake."*

I was hesitant, but acquiesced. Our vacation was a painful, surreal adventure. We zip-lined across the canyons, rode bicycles, sunbathed on the sand, and took in all that the island had to offer.

I also cried enough to fill an ocean. My emotions were raw. I raged at him in private, I wept in front of my children a few times, but mostly pretended normalcy while we filled our time with activities and meals together. And in the early hours of the morning, I slipped away to sit by the ocean while everyone else slept. I felt like an intruder on someone else's vacation with nowhere to hide.

Upon our return, although he agreed to marriage counseling, he refused to stop seeing the other woman. He didn't want me to hate him. I didn't want to hate myself. So, I asked him to make a choice. He did. He moved out a few days later.

Postponing difficult conversations between us had become a habit. But there were things that I needed to know and that would no longer wait. I learned that despite all we had been through, he met someone "easy to talk to, someone who made his world come alive and who brought color back into his dismal, gray existence." That someone wasn't me. And, as if that wasn't enough, he said that he had never truly loved me, that I didn't make him happy. Never had I felt so invisible, so insignificant, or so lost.

My despair was palpable, my pain obvious to everyone around me. I felt such a myriad of emotions, questioning how I could have been so foolish, so unguarded, and so stupid. I was flooded with harsh self-doubt and self-blame.

In the early months, I wasted a lot of time attempting to answer the same question over and over again, "Why?"

I clung to my need to know details that he couldn't articulate, and his awkward attempts to answer only led to more pain for both of us. I was certain that no one could understand or relate to my pain. Believing that no one could understand my grief, and feeling so misunderstood in my anguish, fostered an unbearable isolation and loneliness. After all, he continued to support me financially. As one friend put it, "At least you are getting money. That makes him a stand-up guy."

Yes, having financial support was and is a blessing, and I feel gratitude and humility. This support gave me the space to rebuild my life and to reenter the work world on my terms. Many friends were happily downsizing, retiring, or lightening their workloads at this stage in life. I was starting over. I had no partner and was unsure of my place in the world. I had lost my confidence and my direction.

Even in the twenty-first century, there is shame and embarrassment attached to failing at marriage. I was a single woman. I had failed in marriage and I was starting over. And I admitted this in an interview for a job. Big mistake. I wasn't hired. I had made them uncomfortable.

Perhaps accepting an interview on the day that my divorce was final was not such a good decision.

But I am resilient and resourceful. When I stopped fighting the inevitable and put my resiliency and resourcefulness to work discovering my strengths and talents, I found my life's purpose.

Once I did, the floodgates opened and my life began to change. My marriage was over. The man I had married did not want a life with me. He did not feel happy in my presence. He did not want to rediscover his love for me, because there was no love, only this burning need to escape from me. He packed a few things and left. But not until after we pretended one last time to be a happy family on the worst vacation of my life.

And so we began the dissolution of our marriage. My old life was a closed chapter. In its place, my new life began to take shape, and my spirit began to heal.

I am fortunate to have a supportive therapist, compassionate, empathetic family members and friends, and an abundant library of books to inspire and encourage my personal growth in private at my own pace. These people and resources stood by me through my darkest days, and I borrowed their faith in me until I rekindled my own courage and strength.

I learned to ignore the harsh words of misguided acquaintances who told me how hard they worked to keep their marriages alive, implying that I had somehow failed that "marriage test." Whether true or not, this was the story I told myself. It is more likely they were reassuring themselves of the strength and longevity of their own marriages. Because, after all, if we could get a divorce, what hope was there for anyone else?

Our once beautiful marriage had appeared perfect on the surface. It wasn't. I resented other people for succeeding where I had failed. I blamed my husband. But mostly I blamed myself. I felt shame, embarrassment, and an overwhelming sense of failure.

I could have remained awash in this misery. But a single moment changed my focus and gave me the boost and sense of purpose and clarity that I was missing. While reading Nelson Mandela's words regarding forgiveness, my perception changed. He simply said, *"As I walked out the door toward the gate that would lead to my freedom, I knew if I didn't leave my bitterness and hatred behind, I'd still be in prison."*

I felt humbled by Nelson Mandela's words. Here was a man who had suffered greatly and yet walked away from his captors with a forgiving heart. What was my suffering compared to his? I knew in that moment that unless I chose a path that included forgiveness—of myself and of my husband—I could not fully move forward in my own life and that I would be unsuccessful in modeling wholeness and grounded adulthood. I decided that day that I would fully embrace responsibility for myself and for my future, and this decision has made all the difference to my recovery and happiness.

My need to understand and make sense of this enormous change in my life was a catalyst for reinventing myself and for the recovery of my self-esteem and happiness. I pray that sharing my discoveries will aid you in your healing process and that you, too, will find peace in your storm.

Be well, be hopeful, and prepare to rise from the ashes stronger than ever, six words at a time. Know that the first year *is* the hardest.

~Jennifer

HOW TO USE THIS BOOK

There is one way to read a book like this: *your* way. This book is divided into *52 six-word-titled essays* to savor, one for each week of a whole year.

Read it cover to cover or one essay at a time, a week at a time, or in whatever way you find most useful. Ponder and reflect upon the words, especially the ones that ring true for you. Skip those that don't fit. Write notes in the margins, dog-ear the pages, and use this as a tool to inspire, encourage, and aid your healing process.

TABLE OF CONTENTS

LOSS IS FOREVER,
acute grief fades

LOSS IS FOREVER, ACUTE GRIEF FADES

THE END OF MY MARRIAGE WAS A DEVASTATING LOSS. Gone were my hopes and dreams of what could have been together. Gone forever . . . no turning back. How was I to survive this ache in my heart? Would it, could it get better? Yes.

When my husband left, so did the naïve, hopeful young woman who believed that one plus one did not equal two, but rather infinity. That woman died. I had believed that together we would build something special and wonderful, and had started married life thinking we were on the same page. We were not, and our relationship unraveled ever so slowly from the very beginning, even though I couldn't see it until I looked back.

Ending this journey together felt like such a failure to me, and I grieved the loss acutely. Experts say that acute grief is not infinite, that grief fades even though the loss remains. This idea was impossible for me to believe in the beginning. I felt hopeless, and overwhelmed by my sadness. But there were six words that I heard over and over again. And they gave me hope.

"The first year is the hardest."

I don't remember who said it to me first, but I *do* recall one particular conversation with someone I met by chance while shopping. I was at the fragrance counter at Nordstrom. I stopped to smell the roses, literally. Retail therapy was a baby step that I have since replaced with healthier choices. But at the time, I was lost and looking for something to make me feel better.

I found myself speaking with a kind woman, a little older than me. She was impeccably dressed, confident, articulate. I enjoy one-on-one conversations, and when asked what I was looking for, I answered truthfully! I wanted to find a scent that would re-create the magic and happiness that I had experienced when I was younger. I have always loved fragrance.

The sense of smell powerfully evokes memories and emotions. I tested scents, some that I had worn in the past, but they no longer fit. Interesting, isn't it? I needed something that suited me now, and it wasn't there that day. It would be another year before I discovered my perfect scent.

We spent twenty minutes talking about our children and the journey that had led to divorce. She told me that her *first year was the hardest*!

Inspiration comes at unexpected moments. Here I was feeling vulnerable and invisible . . . looking for something to make me feel feminine and attractive. Instead, I found hope and encouragement. The loss of my marriage was irrevocable. But the acute grief that I experienced faded little by little, over time, until I began to recall happy moments from my marriage without remorse or tears. These were small, welcome victories!

DO
not
BECOME
cold
AS
stone

WEEK 2

DO NOT BECOME COLD AS STONE

I FELT COLD AS STONE, AND FOR A WHILE I LINGERED UNDER THE WEIGHT OF MY SADNESS. When people say, "The days are long, but the years are short," they are often reminiscing and encouraging parents of young children to cherish the little moments, not coaxing a newly divorced woman to stay positive that time will bring her peace. For a while, I forgot to savor the little things. The temptation to hide within my anger and sadness when my life felt so difficult offered solace and a welcome break, but it hampered my health and spirit. I was not cherishing anything in those moments.

In the beginning, my efforts to cope from day to day left no room to appreciate the joy or goodness of my life. I was *not* my best self and focused negatively. I wanted *him* to regret throwing me away. I wanted *him* to regret his hurtful, dismissive words. I wanted *him* to change his mind. It wasn't to be. And so I struggled. Because even though I heard the words of encouragement around me, I didn't believe them, because the days *were* long while I wallowed in self-pity and self-judgment. This negativity made my days longer than they needed to be.

I silently challenged everything, including those fateful words, "The first year is the hardest." I questioned the grammatical correctness of this phrase. Shouldn't we say, "The first year is the most difficult?"

No. And it was always phrased this way, no matter who said it to me. I have come to believe that "hardest" is in fact a fitting choice of words. How easy it would be to become hardened. How tempting to allow it to bury me. I was heading down that path. I feared growing hardened, and yet I had built a wall of protection around me to hide the fact that I was completely crumbling inside.

I found breathing and eating impossible. I remember clearly a day that I forgot to eat. Anyone who knows me knows that I live to eat! So, forgetting would be nearly impossible. Yet I did. I realized about 40 minutes into an intense barre class that I felt lightheaded, and the room began to get a little dark. With every repetition of the challenging exercises I was showing my power and my strength. I imagined *the other woman* feeling intimidated by my presence. I needed to appreciate my power, to connect with my strength, and to use my power for good. And, in that moment, more than anything else, I needed orange juice and a good meal. It was 6 o'clock and I had forgotten to eat all day.

I left the studio, fed myself, and listened once again to my then current favorite Lady Antebellum song, "Cold as Stone."[1] The lyrics felt too familiar and as if written just for me.

---

[1] Lady Antebellum, "Cold as Stone," Sony/ATV Music Publishing LLC, Warner Chapel Music Inc. Released in 2011.

"I wish I was cold as stone . . . I wish I didn't have this heart . . . I wouldn't hurt like this, or feel so all alone . . ."

And in that moment, I decided that I didn't want to remain hardened. I could appreciate the path to writing these lyrics; they were my life in song. But I feared even the idea of becoming hardened would limit my life.

Slowly and bravely, I became open to listening to other people and to hearing their stories and advice. I admitted that I was not alone. I met so many other people starting over again, people who had embarked upon different paths because their partners had opted out, changed their minds, or because they had simply grown apart in their relationships. They all told me the same thing. "The first year is the hardest." I stopped judging their choice of words and just listened.

They shared their struggles and details of what they had overcome. What I saw before me were confident, strong, positive women making a difference in their worlds. Some of them remarried, others chose to remain single. They all exuded an indefinable glow and pride in themselves. I wanted to feel that too.

And so, I allowed the door to open just a little bit and decided that I could do anything for a year. I became guardedly optimistic.

🪷

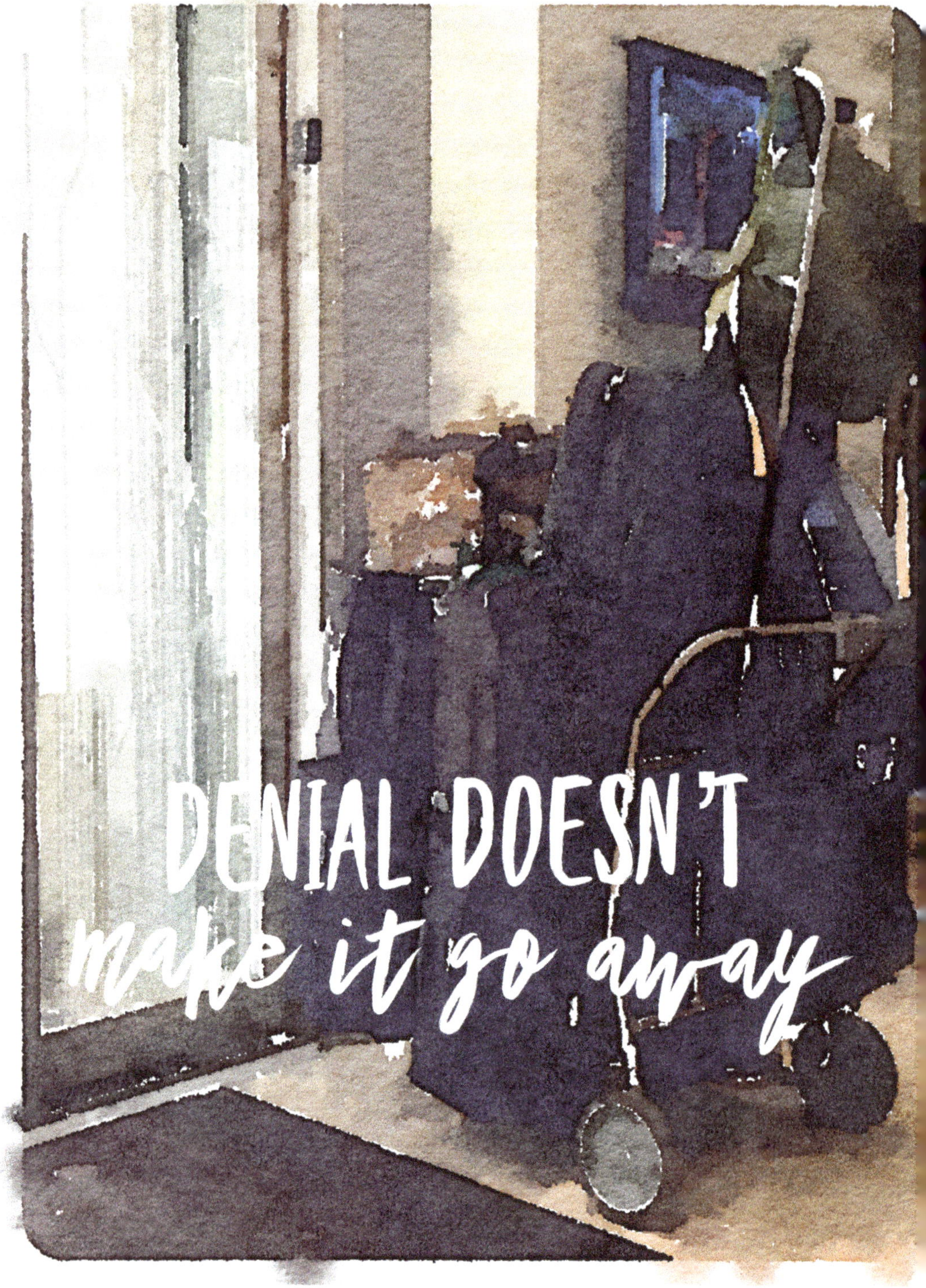
DENIAL DOESN'T
make it go away

DENIAL DOESN'T MAKE IT GO AWAY

DENIAL DOESN'T MAKE ANYTHING THAT EXISTS GO AWAY. The truth is still the truth whether we choose to see it or believe it.

As with any loss, I moved back and forth between the stages of grief. As a nurse, I had witnessed grief daily. Grief is consuming and painful to witness, and I would like to believe that I have offered comfort over the years to the people around me. Yet here I was grieving and unable to wrap my mind around the overwhelming feelings I was experiencing. Had I been sensitive enough to others? I wondered at the hollowness of the comforting words floating around me. They were like a blanket that doesn't quite warm you, but takes the edge off the bitter cold.

And in my efforts to feel warm again, I found denial. It was a safe place to land, giving me respite and a break from the constancy of my heartache. This false attempt to protect me only delayed the inevitable work to be done. I know only too well that just closing my eyes will not make my problems disappear.

I had denied the problems in my marriage by making excuses for behaviors and patterns that were so clearly evidence of disparity. I admitted silently that they existed, but not out loud, and then just as quickly I would find reasons and rationalizations to snuff out my misgivings and doubts.

But everyone has a tipping point or line in the sand. Or, as they say in business, the point of pain, that thing or moment that drives you toward seeking help or service. For me, it was seeing the effect of my husband's indiscretions and self-destructive habits, and the effect that my angry, bitter response to his behaviors had upon our children. I could not ignore or deny this impact. I could no longer cross this line.

And as I truly put my children's needs first, I left denial behind. I didn't have all the answers, but I knew that I *had* to be strong enough to let my husband find his own path. That meant that I had to embrace life as a single woman whether I felt ready or not.

I did it for my children long before I did it for myself. Their needs and my love for them helped me break free from denial. This was another step toward freedom.

Although I thrive on puzzles and challenges, I was now facing the most challenging puzzle of my life. I didn't know where to begin. My sense of overwhelm was enormous. So I did what I ask my clients to do. I lived one moment, one hour, one day at a time. One piece at a time. Taking just one step. And then another.

❋

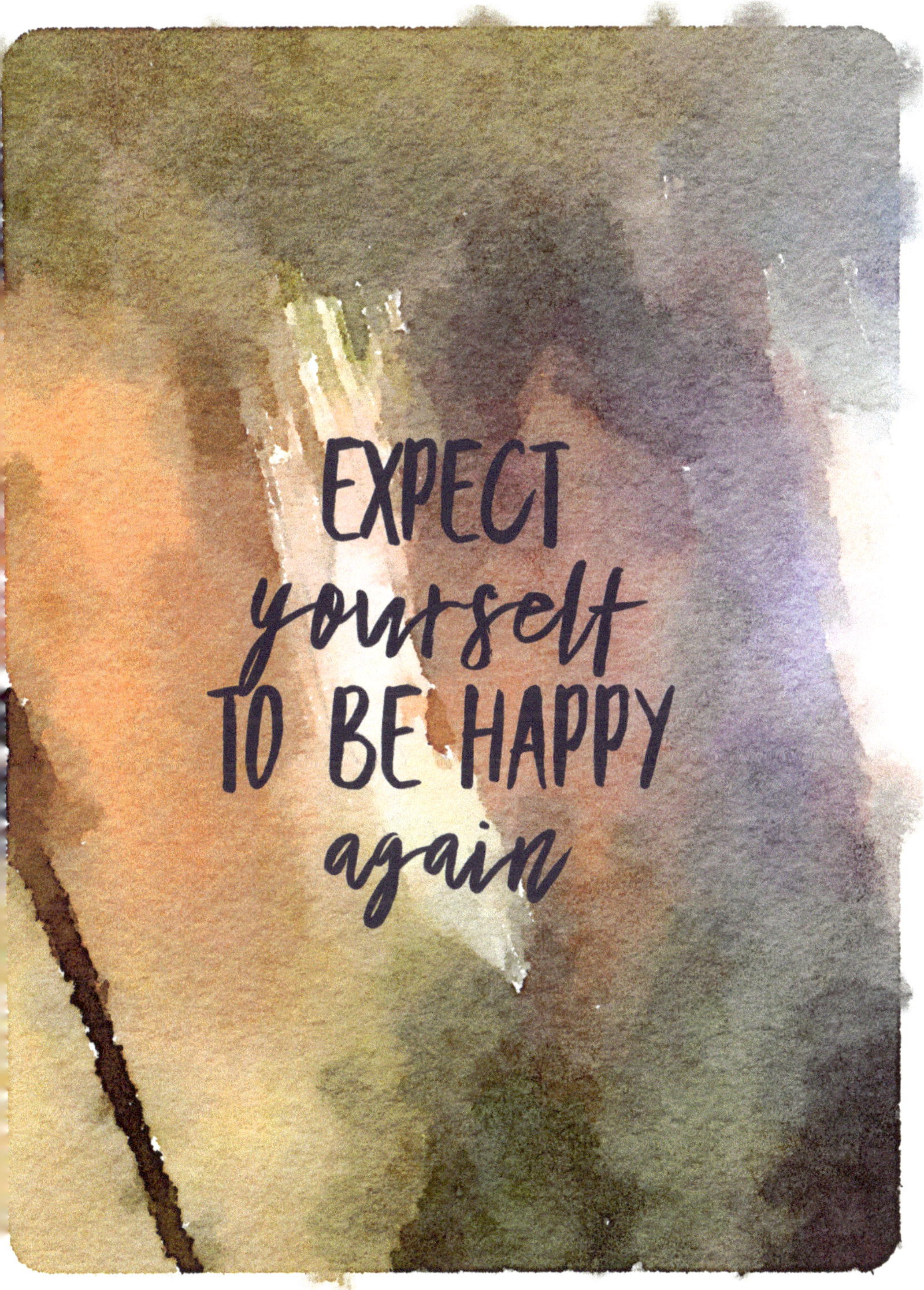
EXPECT
yourself
TO BE HAPPY
again

EXPECT YOURSELF TO BE HAPPY AGAIN

YOU MAY NOT BE READY TO HEAR THIS YET, BUT IT IS IMPORTANT TO KNOW AND BELIEVE THAT YOU WILL BE HAPPY AGAIN. I heard this repeatedly, and at first found it annoying. Who were these people telling me what and how to feel? I could not fathom a day without tears, much less ever feeling truly happy.

Yet, here I sit more than a year later, and the pain *is* less intense, and the moments of happiness and contentedness *are* more frequent. I find these moments while observing the world around me, and in stories.

As for me, I *love* movies! And I find great comfort in repeated viewing of them. It is not that I do not remember their plot lines and stories. I do. Still, I view them each time with new eyes and an open heart. Some might see watching something they have already viewed as a waste of time, but for me, it isn't. I honestly love rediscovering the story and characters again and again.

I enjoy romantic and hopeful stories even though they don't match my life in any way, shape, or form. I find joy in the hopefulness and sentimentality of musical theater and song lyrics like "impossible things are happening every day," lyrics from Rodgers and Hammerstein's *Cinderella*.

I love to quote movie characters, sometimes to the dismay and quandary of the people around me who do not understand my kinship with fictitious characters. But I grew up with books and stories, theater and film, and have never lost my love for the richness that comes from immersing myself in literature and visual arts.

My movie favorites list is endless, but here are six films that I treasure:

1. *My Cousin Vinny* (expect to roar with laughter)

2. *The Proposal* (romantic, funny, and what's not to love with this cast?!)

3. *Under the Tuscan Sun* (just in case you are tempted to move far, far away)

4. *Must Love Dogs* (when considering the absurdity of internet dating)

5. *The Holiday* (because the holidays return every year . . . ready or not)

6. *Love Actually* (expect to cheer for your favorite characters)

Expect to feel joyful. Expect to notice peacefulness and calm in your day and in yourself, and then I urge you to celebrate those moments. Do more of what has brought you to these positive feelings. You are already beginning to heal without even knowing.

I will leave you with lines spoken by Samwise Gamgee, during an emotional scene in our family favorite, "Lord of the Rings."[2] Samwise was and is my favorite character in this story. He was the faithful, humble, steady friend. He offered clarity and hope in confusing and unsettling times. May you find threads of hope and inspiration as I did.

Frodo: *I can't do this, Sam.*

Sam: *I know. It's all wrong. By rights we shouldn't even be here. But we are. It's like in the great stories, Mr. Frodo. The ones that really mattered. Full of darkness and danger, they were. And sometimes you didn't want to know the end. Because how could it end happy? How could the world go back to the way it was when so much bad had happened? But in the end, it's only a passing thing, this shadow. Even darkness must pass. A new day will come. And when the sun shines, it will shine all the clearer. Those were the stories that stayed with you. That meant something, even if you were too small to understand why. But I think, Mr. Frodo, I DO understand. I know now. Folk in those stories had lots of chances of turning back, only they didn't. They kept going. Because they were holding on to something.*

Frodo: *What are we holding on to, Sam?*

Sam: *That there's some good in this world, Mr. Frodo . . . and it's worth fighting for.*

❧

[2] *Lord of the Rings: The Two Towers*, directed and produced by Peter Jackson (2002), screenplay adaptation from J. R. R. Tolkien, *The Two Towers* (1954).

faithless
LOVE
did
I GO
wrong?

WEEK 5

FAITHLESS LOVE, DID I GO WRONG?

Is love faithless? No. Did I go wrong? A more complicated answer haunted me. Yes, no, and maybe.

It is in my nature to blame myself for anything wrong around me and then to try to fix it. I am a fixer. So my failure to maintain a thriving, loving relationship was a blow that I felt deeply. Looking back with a more self-compassionate heart, I ache for that broken spirit and my harsh, unrealistic expectations.

Self-blame requires a tremendous amount of mental energy. I played and replayed every moment and every scenario from 25 years of marriage. I revisited every memory as if I could somehow turn back time and set all to right.

There is very little use in blaming yourself beyond understanding your part in the dance and learning what will lead you toward healthier relationships in your future. There was so much I didn't know and didn't understand about building a healthy relationship. And it takes both people being willing to overcome the obstacles they face in their marriage. Although *I* wanted to save us, he wanted out.

I was awkward and angry and sometimes cruel in reminding my ex-husband of our failures. I resented that I had sacrificed my needs for his for many years. I am not proud of my angry outbursts. And they did nothing to aid my healing process, but rather served to create stagnation and setbacks in the mediation process. My outward anger was a feeble punishment for him not wanting a life with me, and represented my feelings of shame at this perceived failure.

Ironically, he asked me to drive him for shoulder surgery shortly after he moved out of the family home. I asked him why his *new best friend* wasn't driving him, and he said that she didn't know about the surgery. How sanctimonious and righteous I felt in those moments. I let anger become more important than compassion. Although I drove him to his surgery, listened to post-operative instructions, made certain that he was settled and comfortable in his apartment, and checked upon him daily, I was angry and resentful that it was me that he was leaning upon when he had left me for someone else. I had chosen to remain in this subservient role, and then resented him for my choice. I didn't like seeing this side of my nature and felt shame for this digression.

Forgiveness and kindness eventually replaced my anger, and memories of our better selves and happier moments replaced my unpleasant memories. There had been many happy moments and memories of our 25 years together. For a long time choosing to forget them made the loss hurt a little less. I had lost so much when my marriage died. Remembering the goodness softened the sharp edges and made it easier to be genuinely kind to myself and to him.

With practice, we became kinder to each other than we had been in the last years of our marriage. And at the core of everything was the mutual decision to consider our children. It became easier to behave with integrity knowing that their feelings were at stake.

the more you look,
YOU FIND

WEEK 6

THE MORE YOU LOOK, YOU FIND

BLAMING MYSELF WAS UNFAIR AND UNKIND, SO I STOPPED. But I was still looking for answers. Although there are two sides to every story, when I stopped finding fault with my own behavior, I turned outward and laid the blame at his feet.

I read and reread emails and texts that I kept locked in a secret file. These private, personal messages, flirtations, and communications between my ex and the other woman suggesting outings, and plans for meals and time together reminded me that I was no longer important. They also triggered memories of moments when I had felt abandoned by him during our life together.

The fact that he had chosen to connect intimately with someone other than me was a source of great pain, but I was a moth to a flame. I found myself searching the computer for hidden documents and I wasted time searching for what had gone unnoticed until now.

The more I looked for evidence of betrayal, the more I found. Looking back, I know that there was little value in this hunt.

Having a list of wrongdoings did not make things better. It did not bridge the gap. It only served to entrench me in self-pity and self-righteousness. I decided then and there to stop looking for more reasons to feel hurt. I erased the hard drives on the computers and practically gave the computers away to the first person who showed interest in them at a garage sale. I was relieved to let go of them. They had represented the secret life that I didn't share.

I replaced those feelings of self-pity and righteousness with acceptance and compassion for the pain that led to this path that he had chosen. I prayed that he would find health and peace; but I no longer owned his choices. And, I chose to stop equating his choices with my worthiness for love and connection.

I found time for other thoughts and plans. I could be more present in my daily life and notice calm, peace, and pleasure. Even though it wasn't a constant state, it was a habit that began to form. Eventually it took on a momentum of its own.

I now have my first ever personal laptop, purchased by me, chosen by me, and set up by me. It holds none of the negative energy associated with my failed marriage. It represents the progress that I am making in rebuilding and creating my new normal.

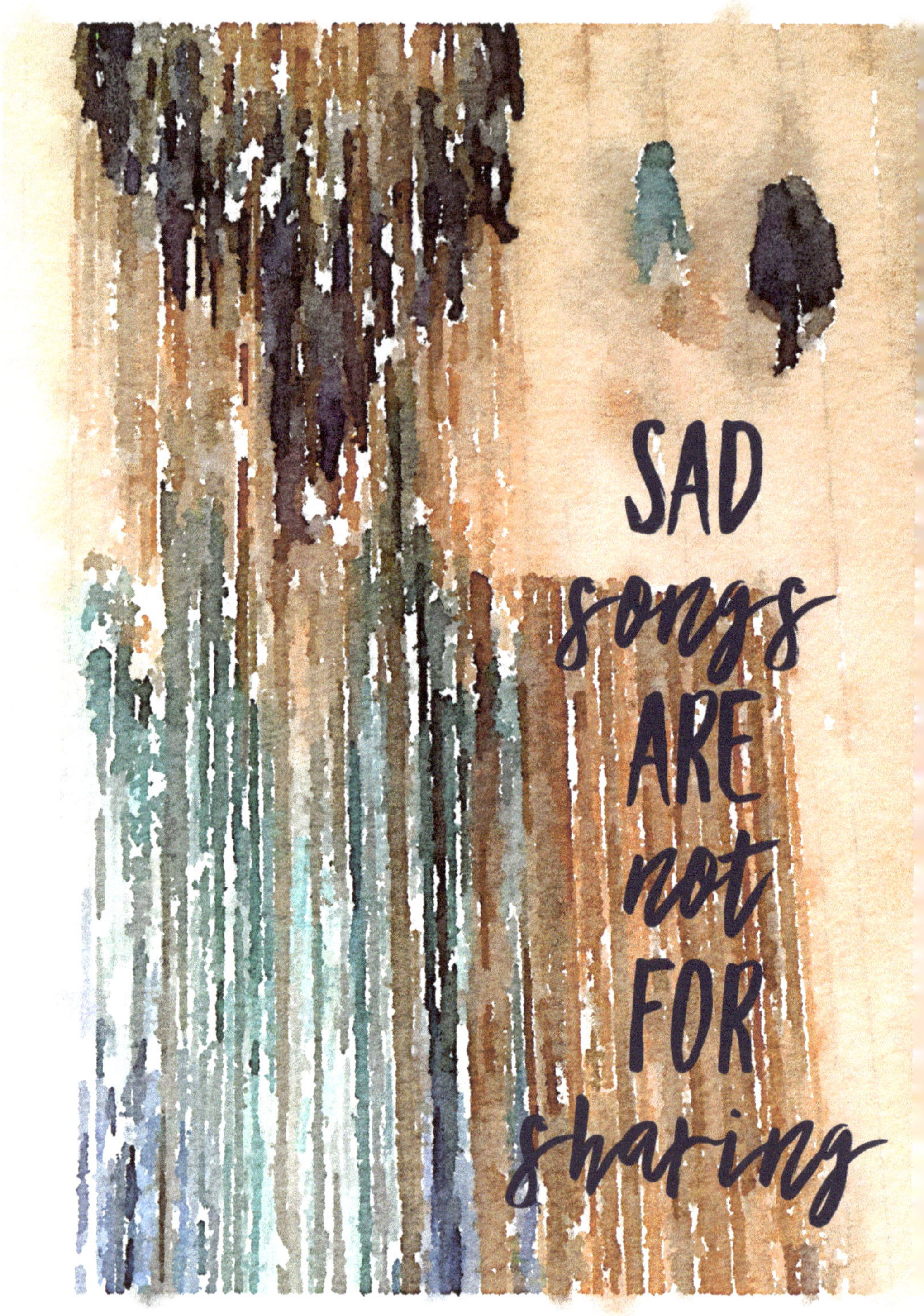
SAD
songs
ARE
not
FOR
sharing

WEEK 7

SAD SONGS ARE *NOT* FOR SHARING

As I left denial behind, I found depression waiting with open arms. I replayed my past relationships all the way back to childhood, particularly high school. And with those mental images came memories of extreme sadness and confusion. I was once again that teenage girl experiencing first love and first heartbreak. Strangely, all these years later, I find comfort and connection with the music from my high school years.

My favorite Linda Ronstadt albums, *Heart Like a Wheel* and *Prisoner in Disguise*, and "Any Day Now: Songs of Bob Dylan" by Joan Baez, were relevant and beautiful armor for me. I added old and new favorite artists to my arsenal: James Morrison, Allen Stone, Amos Lee, Bonnie Raitt, Otis Redding, Miranda Lambert, Lady Antebellum, Alison Krauss, and Adele. My playlist is long, but these artists were my favorites. I knew they understood my pain.

My playlist was one heartbreak song after another: "Love Has No Pride," "Long, Long Time," "Love Is Just a Four-Letter Word," "Fallen Star," "Broken Strings," "Wrong Again," "Things People Say," "Storm Warning," "Circle," "Chill in the Air," "Set Fire to the Rain," and on and on it went.

I played them loudly and repeatedly until the day my son begged me to listen to something else. I continued to listen to my favorite songs, but with headphones and no audience. Sad songs are *not* for sharing with your children.

This not-so-gentle request from my son was a wake-up call for me. Although I was finding comfort with my song choices, I also wondered if they allowed me to wallow a little bit too much. With this thought came another . . . what if I shift toward more uplifting and powerful lyrics? Would I feel empowered and strengthened?

The answer to these questions became clearer as the days progressed: "Yes!"

your children are
SUFFERING AS WELL

WEEK 8

YOUR CHILDREN ARE SUFFERING AS WELL

I WAS HUMBLED AND ASHAMED TO REALIZE HOW SELFISH AND SELF-AB-SORBED I HAD BECOME. When your son says, "Mom, I cannot listen to one more sad song," you have burdened him and certainly his introverted and extremely private sister who is quieter and fiercely guards her feelings. *These marital changes in my life were changes in their lives as well.* How ashamed I felt, realizing that I had added to their grief. Yet I had.

Thankfully, my son was vocal about his distress and was willing to share his discontent with me. My daughter followed suit, telling me that I was oblivious to her suffering. I felt the sting of their words deeply, yet they were words I needed to hear.

Neither of them wanted anything to do with psychotherapy, even though it came highly recommended by the mediating attorney.

Rather than force my timeline upon them, I went to work on myself first. I figured if it is important to "don your own oxygen mask first" in the event of loss of cabin pressure and change in oxygen levels while flying, then it should be equally important to discover my own path for healing, and to model those changes for my children.

I found that as I worked through my own grief, I became happier and more content with the new course of my life, bumps and bruises and all. I know that it showed. Friends remarked that I was "different, in a good way."

Although it was important for my children to see my honesty, they also needed my honesty to be tempered with strength and a willingness to grieve in private when it was too much for them to bear.

You may discover, as I did, that the healthier your own outlook and outward appearance, the happier your children become. "Fake it till you make it," as they say. They are suffering too, and it helps them when you are happy. It gives them permission to be happy too.

I asked mine to continue to be honest with me as I forged my way through uncharted waters for us toward a calm, stable home life considering their needs, but mine as well.

MUSIC and LYRICS A common CONNECTION

MUSIC AND LYRICS, A COMMON CONNECTION

ALTHOUGH I FOUND TRUE COMFORT FROM MY MUSIC CHOICES, I ALSO FELT EXPOSED. I have always connected with music on a visceral level. During the first days on my own, I felt a kinship with the songwriters and those who sang my life and my pain. I was moved by their vulnerability, and when I looked past my own hurt, I came to understand that these songs were not an exposure of *my* pain but of theirs, which brings to light how common heartache and heartbreak are.

I am forever grateful to the artists who exposed their feelings and gave voice to words I could not articulate. And, as I gravitated to more uplifting, powerful lyrics, I felt empowered by a new energy and resiliency.

I listened, and still do, to many different artists. I listen to everything from "Turn Down for What" by DJ Snake and Lil Jon, to "Love Will

Find You Again" by Claire Lynch, to "Fighter" by Christina Aguilera, to "Please Don't Stop the Rain" by James Morrison.

I listened to my music repeatedly along my winding path until the music and lyrics became my own. My eclectic mix of melodies and lyrics has the power to calm me when I feel agitated, to lift my spirits when I feel sad, and to comfort me when I feel alone in my grief.

I also remembered how much I love being a part of a music group, and a new goal sprang to life. I had *always* been a part of a music group in some form or fashion from a very young age. To say that I gave it up for marriage is not completely truthful. I did not know how to have both, so I left my musical aspirations to immerse myself completely in my new married life.

Two months to the day after our wedding day, I found myself living in another country away from everyone who knew this musical side of me, and so days turned to years of singing alone in the car and lullabies to my babies, until I was shushed by my spouse, who didn't understand how I could sing the same song over and over again. I was embarrassed and stopped singing in front of anyone for a very long time, and when asked to sing, found excuses to say no rather than embarrass myself. I had lost my confidence and the joy of singing because I let someone else's opinion of me matter more than my own.

I didn't realize how much I missed singing for its own sake until I was asked to sing at a friend's wedding about a year after my divorce became final. Since then I have been relearning to play the guitar, song lyrics and chords, and exploring new music. I play my song choices repeatedly, to my heart's content. It feels good.

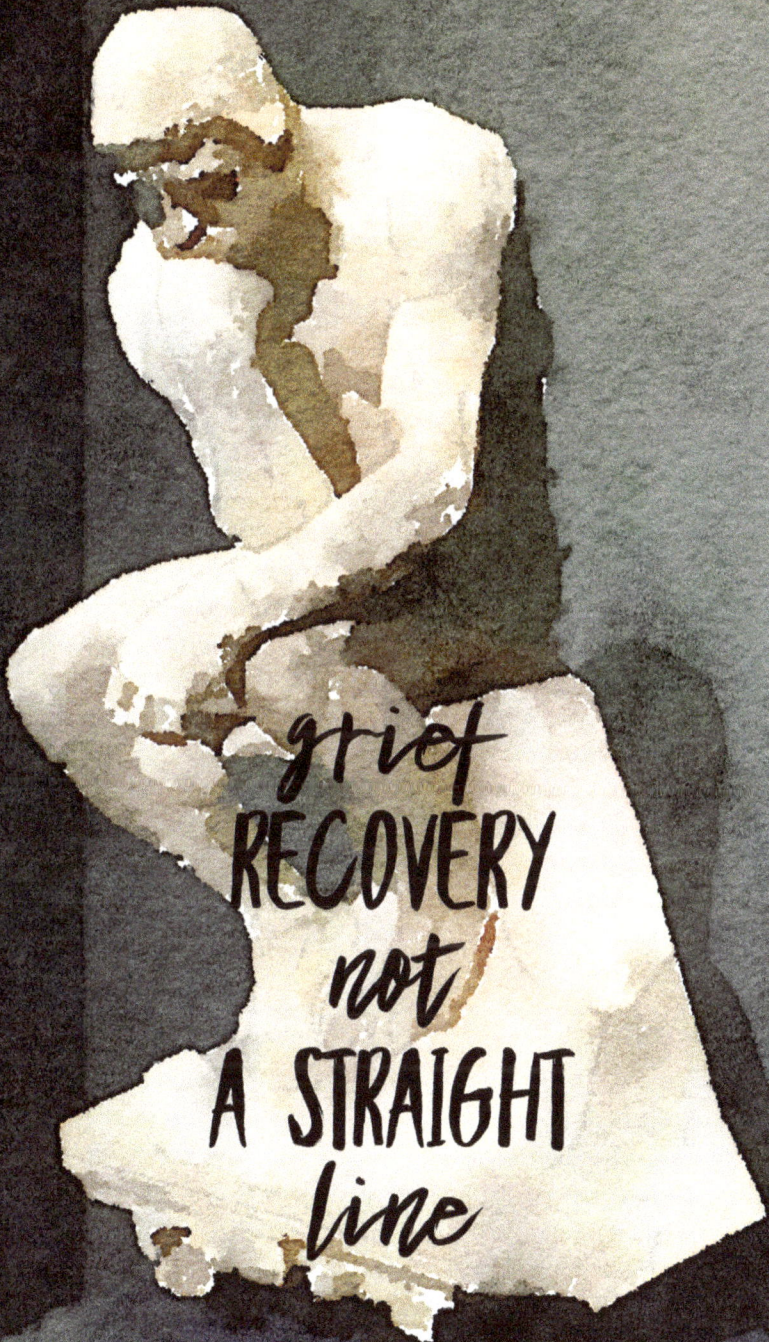

grief
RECOVERY
not
A STRAIGHT
line

WEEK 10

GRIEF RECOVERY, NOT A STRAIGHT LINE

MANY BOOKS HAVE BEEN WRITTEN ABOUT GRIEF AND ITS DIFFERENT STAGES. What I had failed to appreciate until now is how often we move back and forth between the stages: denial/isolation, bargaining, anger, depression, acceptance. Recovery is *not* a straight line. It took me on a winding, dizzying, circuitous path.

For months, all but acceptance seemed to fight for my attention. I went back and forth and round and round. It took self-compassion and a sense of humor to combat these feelings.

It was during the early months that I opened up to a few people who were just strangers to me, in my life for a brief time, who noticed my pain and offered advice and compassion. My willingness to really listen to what they said to me required humility and patience. I didn't have the answers and I needed to stop judging myself. What I know for certain is that it is unhealthy to judge these confusing emotions too harshly. In such a difficult time, emotions are real and potent outlets.

Although unexpected at the time, looking back I am not surprised that I found strength in the studio where I practiced ballet-inspired barre exercise. I had a secret desire to be an ice dancer when I was a little girl. I remember poring over the Sears catalog as a young girl, looking at pink tights and tutus, imagining myself spinning and twirling. I had no idea of the tremendous effort and hours of training involved. I just knew that it looked beautiful.

Ironically, my daughter studied dance for several years. After suffering a painful stress fracture during training, she was encouraged to regain her core strength through barre classes. Being the shy young woman she was, she needed a training partner. I became that partner.

What a blessing in disguise! Of course, she became stronger and returned to dancing. And I discovered a new form of exercise that really fit me. I got to wear dancewear, and I became fitter than I thought possible. And I did it with my daughter, who I adore, and with some of the most encouraging and inspirational women I know. They encouraged me from my first day at the studio and continue to inspire me.

Perhaps some of these women could see in my face what they them-selves had experienced and overcome. I see it in others now and wonder if that is how I looked a year ago. No matter the reason, I am so grate-ful for the solidarity of women, as well as the men raised by strong women who also shared their stories with me.

I borrowed from their beliefs and their hopefulness until I felt stronger. Although it took time to get there, I was sensing the line beginning to straighten out just a bit, and could see a faint glimmer of hope and light.

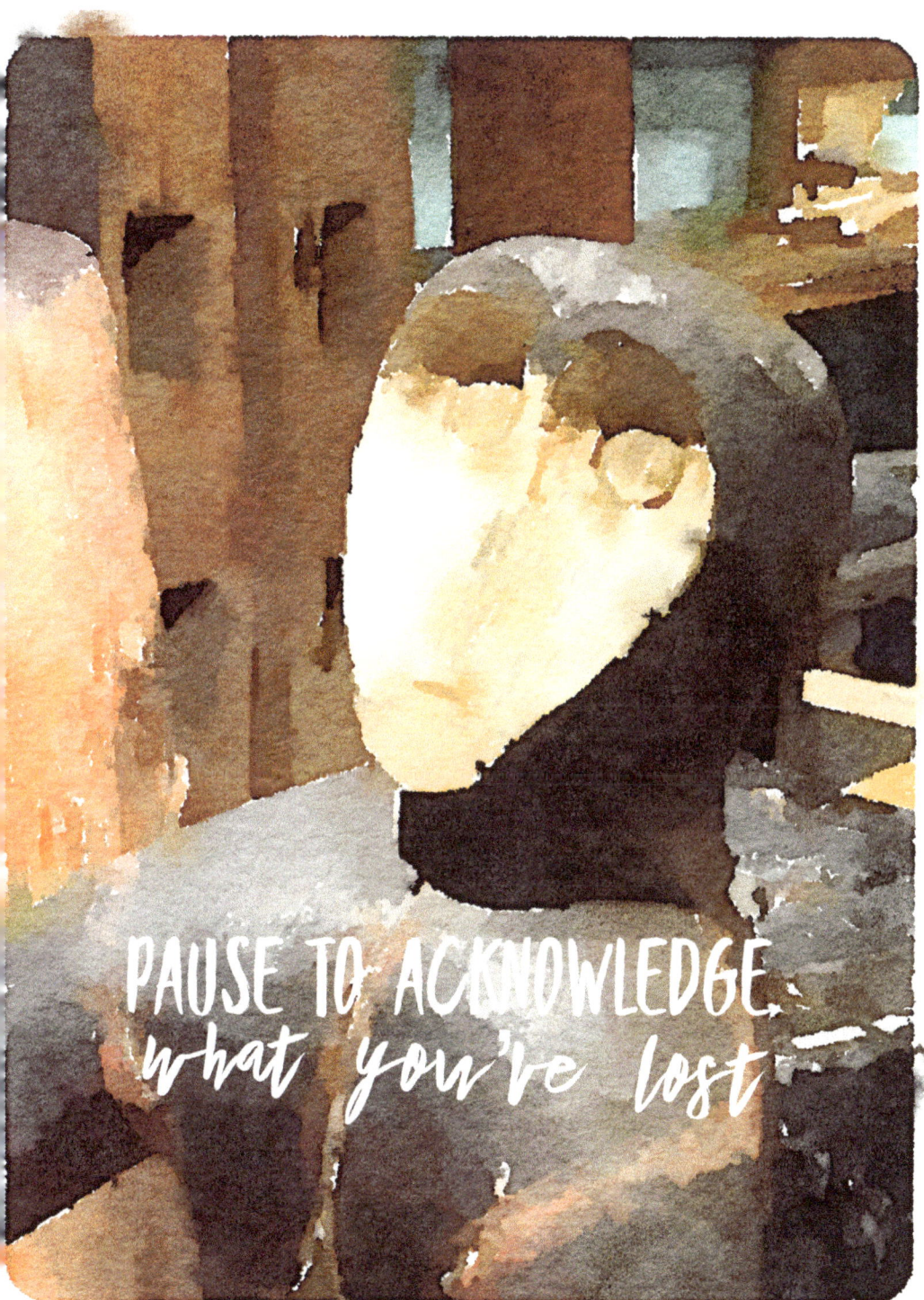

PAUSE TO ACKNOWLEDGE
what you've lost

PAUSE TO ACKNOWLEDGE WHAT YOU'VE LOST

I AGONIZED OVER WHAT I HAD LOST. I focused upon the negatives: the loss of a dream of a life together, the loss of a partner to share in life's trials and tribulations, the loss of stability and a harmonious view of a bright future. I could only see shattered dreams, physical and emotional instability, and shifting family dynamics.

Whether you mend your relationship or you move on to a new life without your partner, there will be changes that are permanent. This knowing felt overwhelming to me. I cried enough to fill an ocean, and then moved on to angry outbursts, feelings of bitterness and denial, and everything in between.

As immersed as I was in these feelings, I wanted to feel more than loss in my life. Could acknowledging my losses allow me to move forward? As I paused to reflect upon this, I found myself borrowing language that I use in my business practice.

"Keep what you need, what you use, and what you love while being mindful of the boundaries and space that are available to you." Simple, but not always easy.

I am a professional organizer. I encourage my clients to let go of the stuff in their homes that no longer serves a purpose in their lives. I also encourage them to pause and cherish the newly open and empty spaces before rushing to fill them with more stuff.

Deep down inside, I knew that I needed to take these same steps. I had been living with a tremendous amount of stress and emotional and physical clutter in my married life. Letting go of a marriage that no longer worked felt like I imagine jumping off a cliff and expecting to sprout wings would feel. Reckless. Uncertain. Risky! Yet as I look back, it was the only and obvious choice. Who knew that the person waiting at the bottom of my fall would be me, catching myself, picking myself up, dusting myself off, and getting on with my new life.

I can see now that I was letting go of what was no longer working and making space for something different to enter my life. I prefer an orderly, calm home environment, and I have that now. Knowing that at the end of a long workday I can return to my calm home to rejuvenate, reflect, and reset, feels like such a blessing.

It is during these pauses that I acknowledge what I have lost, and what I have gained as well: an open, empty canvas to paint the next chapters of my life, acknowledging that the process of growth and change is a lifelong journey, not a destination.

❧

RESENTMENT
blocks
THE
path
TO CONTENTMENT

WEEK 12

RESENTMENT BLOCKS
THE PATH TO CONTENTMENT

ONE EMOTION THAT PLAGUED ME TIME AND TIME AGAIN WAS RESENTMENT. My trigger point was simple. All it took was for a day to feel challenging in any way, and my knee-jerk reaction was immediately to blame him for whatever struggle I was facing. What followed would be a mental replay of the disintegration of my marriage and a surge of negative energy.

I wasted a lot of energy looking backward and wishing that things could have been different. But what I resented most was the loss of what I thought were my "best years." I anguished over his poor choice of words, particularly the day he told me that he had never loved me and that he had "just settled for me." Who wants to be someone's second choice? Did his doubts lead to our lack of harmony?

How many times had I attempted to talk to him about my unsettling, nagging feeling that something was amiss in our relationship. At first, he would say it was nothing. Over time the message changed to, "It's all in your head." And eventually he told me if it bothered me, I should get help, but that *he* didn't need it.

I resented the absence of a true connection, and that despite my efforts to reach out, he would not or could not meet me halfway. I had craved his love and attention and had remained faithful to our vows. Only my best friend knew how lonely and empty the final years of my marriage were. She guarded my secret and listened patiently to my repeated rants, which must have been a heavy burden for her.

Resentment is tiresome; it had drained me, body and soul. Even now, I struggle with it as I anticipate selling the home where I raised my children. My son no longer lives with me, but my daughter does.

As much as I love the view out my back window and the peacefulness of the spaces around me, and as much as I anguish over uprooting my daughter from the safety and comfort of what is familiar to her, I know that it is time to unburden us all from the weight of the past.

Letting go of resentment has allowed me to feel gratitude and contentment with my progress. It allows me to focus my energies where they do their best work, toward healing my soul and rebuilding and appreciating my life, and leads me toward truly standing on my own two feet. Letting go of the family home without resentment is the final, healing, albeit painful release.

I believe that in making this change, I am making room for something else, not necessarily better, but good nonetheless. I am excited and nervous as I anticipate establishing my new nest, and will embrace the challenges that this will inevitably bring.

※

yes, i swore
LIKE A SAILOR

WEEK 13

YES, I SWORE LIKE A SAILOR

I WAS A PRESSURE COOKER FOR A WHILE, AND THE WAY THAT I VENTED WAS BOTH THROUGH EXERCISE, A HEALTHY OUTLET, AND, I AM EMBARRASSED TO ADMIT, THROUGH SWEARING.

Although unattractive, swearing was an outlet that I found wholly satisfying. Swearing was new to me. It wasn't part of my upbringing. Yet I found new and inventive ways to express myself, and I justified my frequent use of the multiplicity of expletives by telling myself that it was necessary to express the depth of my emotions. To say that my colorful language matched my colorful emotions would be a self-compassionate understatement.

Brené Brown writes about forgiveness and anger in her book, *Rising Strong*. She quotes Archbishop Tutu, who says, "The depth of your love is shown by the extent of your anger."[3] I stopped dead in my tracks

3 Brené Brown, *Rising Strong* (New York: Random House, 2017), 151.

when I read those few words. It rang so true for me and shed light on my need to express my anger. But, I realized as I read her book, I still had feelings for my ex and knew my feelings were unreciprocated. This was a source of embarrassment and despair. And it appeared in the form of many four-letter words.

I cringe now when I recall my lapse of decorum and offer these words of caution . . . if you are going to swear like a sailor, be prepared to shock a few people and lose a few friends. You will discover who cares about you. Your truest friends will still be there when the dust settles. And you will wake up one day, as I did, and realize that you are happy and the f-bomb is no longer your first-line-of-defense adjective.

As my anger dissipated, the shock value of swearing wore off. I sensed the people around me became more relaxed in my presence. I am no longer angry that *he* doesn't love me. I have moved on. I am even hopeful that there is love waiting for me in my future. And I will be comfortable expressing myself the next time around. The next man in my life will know the depth of my emotions.

be cautious of
YOUR NEGATIVE THOUGHTS

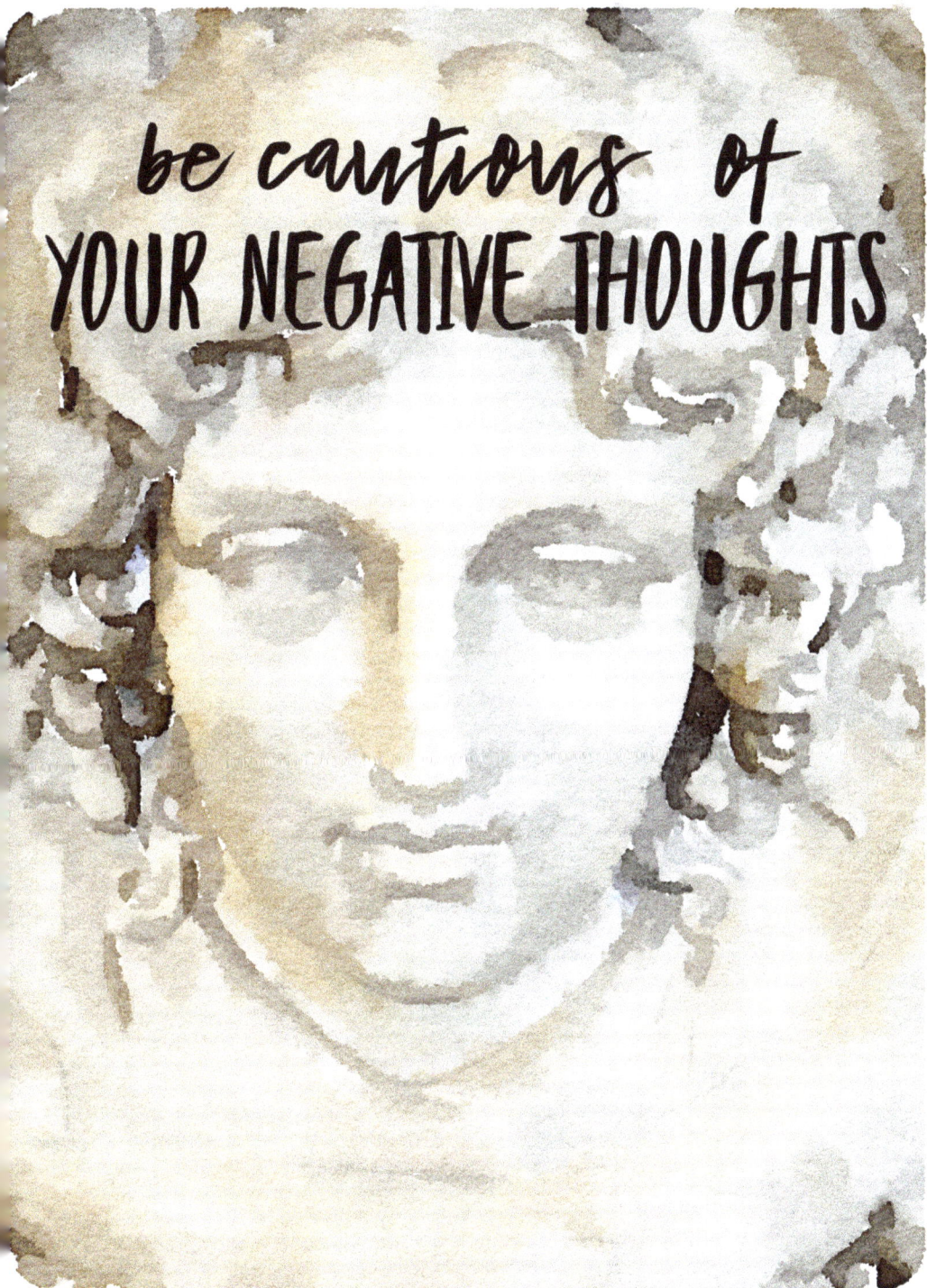

WEEK 14

BE CAUTIOUS OF
YOUR NEGATIVE THOUGHTS

"Avoid negative thoughts." These were the first words of advice I received from several sources, including the psychic whose wisdom I sought at the urging of a trusted advisor (thank you, Shelley).

Yes! I admit that I called a psychic healer, desperate to hear words of encouragement, to hear someone tell me that things would be okay and that I would wake up unscathed from this nightmare. She was kind, empathetic, and insightful. And she was guarded in her optimism for reconciliation.

In the months that followed our separation, negative thoughts clouded my thinking frequently and became an invitation to wallow in self-pity. On days that I entered that negative space, I sought the people who would tell me what I wanted to hear.

They would agree that I had every reason to feel sad, mad, blah, blah. Thankfully, there were also people around me who challenged my way of thinking. They saw the light just past my hurt and anger. I learned to listen to them and at least consider the option of finding a positive thought to replace the negative ones.

With practice, this became easier and easier; reframing my life in a more positive tone took on a life of its own. And, the happier I became, the happier my children became. And weren't they my raison d'etre, my reason for living, at this point?!

🪷

AVOID FOCUS ON
seduction of inadequacy

WEEK 15

AVOID FOCUS ON SEDUCTION OF INADEQUACY

WHEN LUPITA NYONG'O ACCEPTED HER ACADEMY AWARD FOR *12 YEARS A SLAVE*, SHE SPOKE OF THE SEDUCTION OF INADEQUACY. She described her years of struggle with feeling invisible and believing she was less than worthy because of her skin color.[4]

I cried throughout her speech. I cried for the little girl who felt unworthy. I cried as I applauded her triumph in overcoming the cruelties of racism and the nonsensical social limitations on beauty. And I cried for myself, as I recognized that I had become seduced by my own perceived inadequacies.

---

4   "Black Girl Magic Flashback: Watch the Lupita Nyong'o Speech Heard Around the World," *Essence* Magazine, February 27, 2014, http://www.essence.com/2014/02/27/lupita-nyongo-delivers-moving-black-women-hollywood-acceptance-speech.

I had allowed the end of my marriage to define my worthiness as a person for a long time. But no more. My eyes opened to the possibility of a new path that included self-compassion and the rebuilding of my self-worth.

My ex-husband and I were no longer building a life together. It became critical for me to recognize my own significance as I veered toward the path of my new life. I needed to define the criteria that measure my success. I no longer needed more than my own approval.

It was at this point that I began to resent the people in my life who would smugly tell me how hard they had worked on their own relationships or would relate a story of someone much worse off than I, implying that I wasn't counting my blessings. My brain understood that well-intentioned friends and acquaintances were thinking about their own relationships or were attempting to offer solace and advice. But it just served to feed my feelings of inadequacy. My heart translated their words to mean that I had not tried hard enough, and this fostered my feelings of shame.

I found myself justifying my life and sharing more of my story than I trusted them to honor. I felt an overwhelming need to be understood, but would immediately regret this painful retelling of my story when I was so ready to move forward.

I learned to recognize a passive-aggressive speech pattern from people who thought they were being helpful. Encouragement often began with the words, "Well, at least . . ." The more often I heard these words, the more they made me cringe. I wonder how often I have used the same insulting phrase, and I now make every effort not to use it when speaking to others.

I have learned to be more honest about what I need when speaking to others. Noticing the speech patterns that trigger resentment and feelings of inadequacy, stopping them before I feel shame, and redirecting the conversation toward a healthier outlook have become powerful habits.

BORROW BELIEF FROM those around you

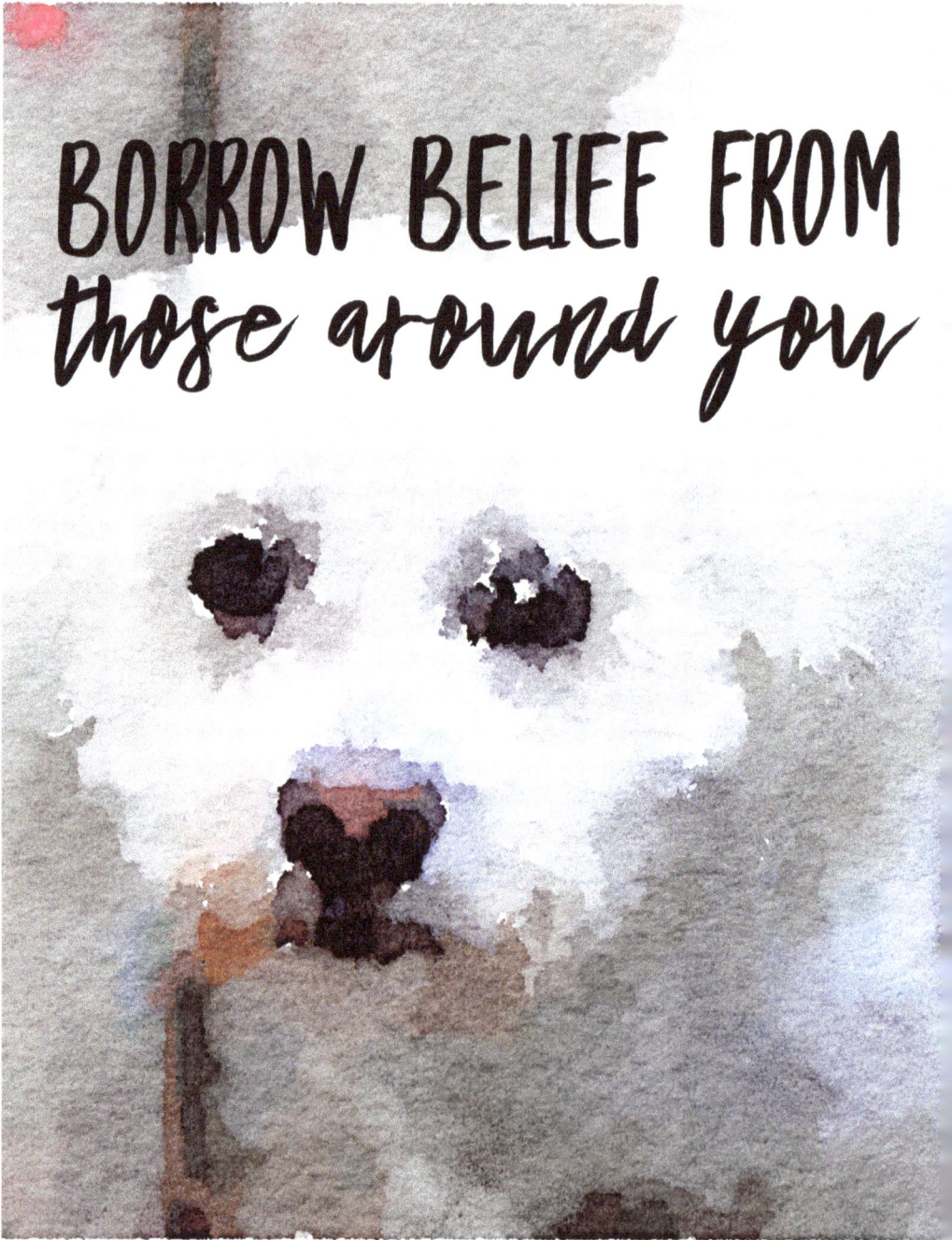

BORROW BELIEF FROM THOSE AROUND YOU

SOME DAYS I WOKE UP FEELING READY TO TAKE ON THE WORLD. I felt confident and optimistic. But there were many days when I felt weak and uncertain. These were the days I borrowed strength from the people around me, from those I trusted the most, and from those who showed confidence and spirit in their life choices. I sought them out. I surrounded myself with like-minded people who were setting the world on fire. I watched what they were doing and what set them apart.

I read every book recommended to me, looking for a glimmer of hope and pearls of wisdom that might show me what to do next. I read *Daring Greatly*, *Rising Strong*, and *The Gifts of Imperfection*, all written by Brené Brown. I read Amy Cuddy's book, *Presence*, and *Mindset*, by Carol S. Dweck. These authors inspired me to stand strong and believe in myself.

I continued to read daily to support my personal growth. And I pored over references regarding business growth and development to understand how to best serve the people who would become my clients. My business was no longer just an idea. I was committed to bringing it to life, believing in its possibility for me.

I have always loved organizing and "setting up," as we called it when I was a girl. Here I was reorganizing my life, sorting and redesigning my spaces to suit the life I have now and to inspire the life I am seeking. Could I do this professionally? I knew that I could, and my business, Less-Stress Organizing Solutions, was born from a moment of confidence that the world needs what I am good at.

From then on, I found that everything was connected. My personal growth and development fostered my work development, and vice versa.

I discovered Pinterest and established many boards that inspire me and that support my work. I love the creativity of this tool. It is as portable as my cell phone. I have my visual inspirations close at hand, and I read and review posts and pictures that are positive, encouraging, and motivating every day. I encourage my clients to create boards to inspire and motivate them as well.

Although believing in myself was slow to grow, when others told me, "You will become whole again. You are worthy of happiness and love," I borrowed their belief in me until it became my own.

Maybe others sense something we cannot yet see. They have been our confidants, friends, and mentors, on paper and in person. I trust and believe that we are all capable of building something important and beautiful.

And we *are* worthy of happiness and love!

BE
strong,
FIND
patience,
TRUST
yourself

BE STRONG, FIND PATIENCE, TRUST YOURSELF

STARTING OVER IS A SCARY, YET EXCITING SPACE TO LIVE IN. It is overwhelming, and it threatens your sanity. So many decisions and choices fought for my attention, and I struggled with self-doubt. I lacked the confidence to trust the decisions I was making.

There were a few choices that I made early on that helped me to find patience when self-doubt reared its ugly head. I accepted that I would make mistakes but that I would learn from them. It became easier not to have all the answers when I let go of perfectionism. I slept better as a result, and no longer lay awake at night reviewing solutions to all the possible scenarios playing in my head. This was so liberating.

I surrounded myself with lots of different people. I asked them questions, and I studied how they worked. I stopped feeling threatened by our differences and decided to become interested in how these differences interplayed. Attending the SUE Talks in San Diego was a pivotal evening for me. Although crowds are stressful for me, I attended to support a friend. I heard amazing stories from women who are thriving in their lives despite what could have been insurmountable obstacles. I felt inspired by all of them.

I looked at the big picture both behind me and in front of me when the minutiae of the day overwhelmed me. Appreciating my progress and knowing my goals are a part of my lifelong journey allows me to savor the present moment. I became more patient with the process.

I avoided self-talk that included the words "always" and "never." Why tempt fate?!

I learned to trust my gut. I am uncomfortable in a large group. By large, I mean more than three people. One-to-one counseling was a perfect fit for me. That said, I gave in to pressure from a trusted resource and joined a marriage support group to accelerate the growth and healing process. Having divorce in common did not forge an immediate bond with me in such a setting.

My anxiety doubled. I lost sleep worrying about the people in my group. I worried about how much information I had shared with these strangers, and found I could not be authentic because I worried about their responses to my story. My gut told me that this group setting wasn't a good fit for me. Despite the urgings of the group, I left it to resume counseling in the way that worked best for me and never regretted this decision.

Every time I honor my gut and trust myself, I become stronger. Ironically, the less I worry about feelings of impatience, the more patient I become.

❀

DISCOVER your BEACH, your storm HAVEN

WEEK 18

DISCOVER YOUR BEACH, YOUR STORM HAVEN

In the moments, days, and weeks that felt the stormiest, where I felt at odds and impatient with myself and with coping with my aloneness, it became important to have a haven of sorts, a place that calmed me.

Mine was the beach.

There is something magical about sand and salt water and the sounds of the sea. Author Isak Dinesen once said, "The cure for anything is salt water: sweat, tears or the sea."[5] I have certainly found this to be true.

---

5   As quoted in *Reader's Digest* (April 1964). See also Isak Dinesen, *Seven Gothic Tales* (New York: Vintage Books, 2011), 39.

How fortunate am I that I can drive, park, and be sitting at the water's edge in half an hour. No matter how agitated or irritable I feel, I cannot resist the lull of repeated waves crashing around me.

The sound is deafening, and when I listen to the music of the crashing waves, my breathing slows down. This alters my sense of well-being, and allows me to stop the endless chatter in my head and to be fully present in the moment. This is my favorite form of meditation.

At first, it would take an hour or more of sitting quietly on the beach before I would give in to this peacefulness. Eventually I would relax, often drifting off to sleep. Now, just the thought of the beach or the sight of the coastline has the same calming effect on me, and I keep a few seashells on my mantel to remind me of this treasured place.

Finding a safe space or haven is important to me. And it is important to visit it often.

I have passed this on to my clients and love hearing about how they connect with their environments in truly personal ways. One client has added color throughout her home by painting her walls and furniture in her favorite colors, because color adds joy to her life. Another has added what we refer to as her "Kathy Corner." When her daughter comes home to visit, they sit in this space and reminisce and sort through boxes of treasures together. I *love* that!

❁

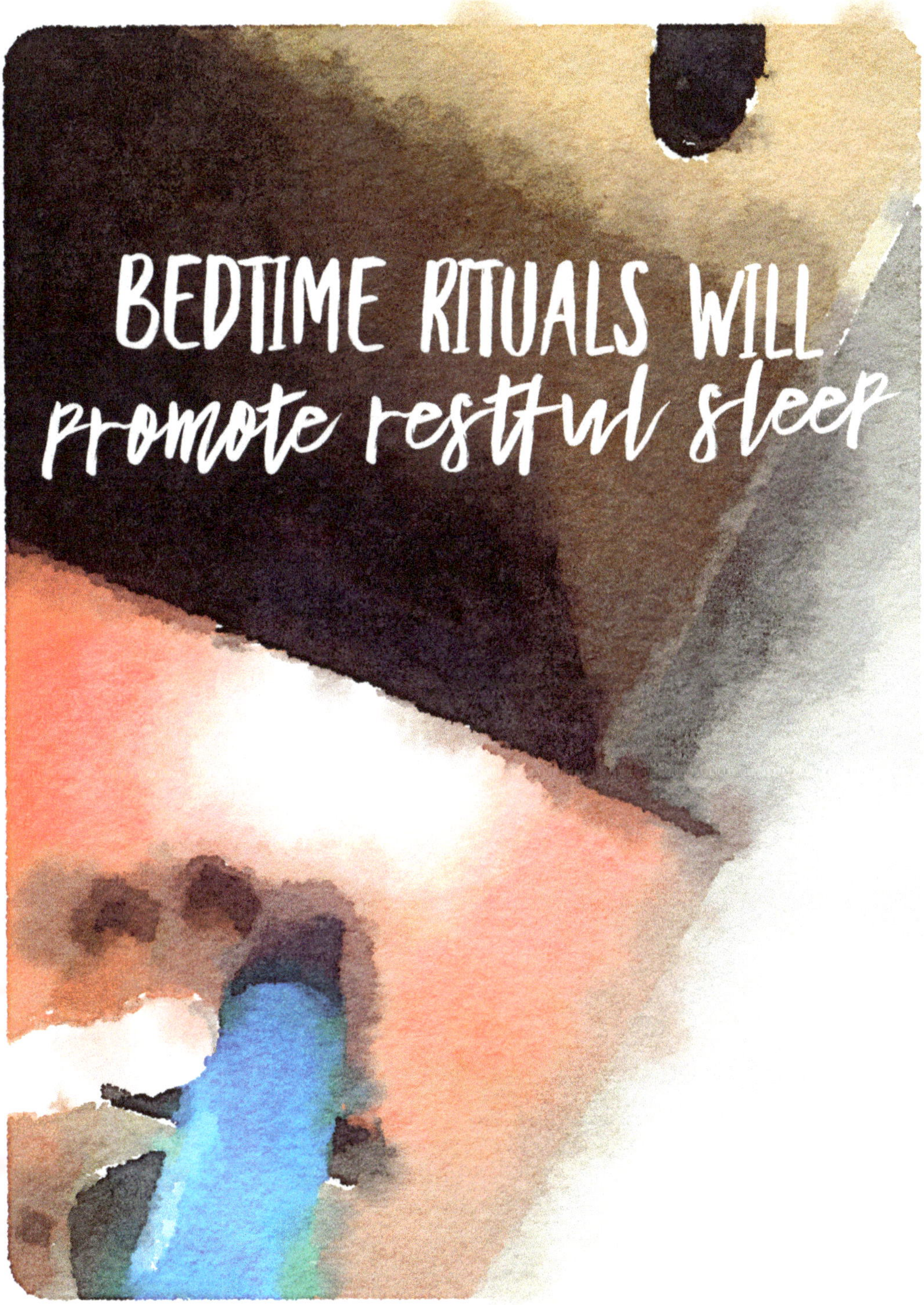
BEDTIME RITUALS WILL
promote restful sleep

WEEK 19

BEDTIME RITUALS WILL PROMOTE RESTFUL SLEEP

As daytime became more manageable, I found comfort in my routines.

But then it would happen! Bedtime . . . the dreaded quiet and aloneness in the dark where my fears and doubts threatened to drown me. Sleep was elusive.

Restful, deep, uninterrupted sleep has been pivotal in my recovery. It is one of the most important elements of healthy living according to countless resources, including my personal physician. I am now witness to the power of regular, restful sleep.

I did not know how sleep-deprived I had become until I had a few full nights of sleep. Oh, how this changed my attitude and my outlook! I had more energy and could truly focus my energy during the day.

I stopped lying in bed worrying about what was outside of my control. I still cared about where my children were and what they were doing, but I acknowledged I could not control the outcome of their outings by worrying. I still cared about decisions that I was making and what was coming next. But it is exhausting to consider all possibilities and then all possible solutions. My perspective shifted when I let go of this impossible task.

I decided that even if something terrible happened I could better meet the challenge if I was fully rested. I gave myself permission to sleep. This decision aided my sleep tremendously, and I am better equipped to meet the challenges of the day.

As I developed simple bedtime rituals and routines, my sleep improved. Each night, I pass through my home room by room putting things away, starting the dishwasher and a load of laundry, adjusting tomorrow's to-do list, shutting off lights, closing blinds, and letting the dog outside one more time. Then I head upstairs with a freshly brewed cup of herbal tea and a book, or to watch a favorite movie. I rarely last 15 minutes before I am drifting off to deep, restful sleep.

I do this every night, no matter what. I *love* falling asleep knowing that there is a sense of order in my home that will greet me in the morning. Simple. Mundane, really, but together these steps signal that the day is coming to a close and that it is time to sleep. And I *do*.

let friends bring
COMFORT AND JOY

LET FRIENDS BRING COMFORT AND JOY

DESPITE MY BEST EFFORTS, WHETHER I FELT RESTED OR NOT, THERE WERE DAYS WHEN I FELL OFF THE RAILS. A few months after my ex-husband moved out, I had such a day.

I had registered to take an important test for a business credential only to realize that it fell on the same day as my daughter's final dance competition. This would be her last year to compete, so my decision to postpone the test was an easy one. Watching her beautiful dancing was bittersweet, knowing that she was growing up and that this phase of her life was closing.

This dance event occurred early in our separation, and I wasn't ready to sit beside my ex and reminisce about our daughter's dance journey. I wanted space away from him and I wanted to sit with my dance mom friends. But I felt compelled to look out for his feelings and well-being in an environment I knew he was uncomfortable in.

I did not welcome the pressure I put upon myself to help him fit in and ease his anxiety. This left me moody, irritable, and emotionally exhausted.

Despite my bad mood, my friends sought out my company at lunchtime. You have got to love friends who don't let you wallow and won't leave you out of what they consider to be "the fun!" I reluctantly joined them for lunch, but honestly didn't expect any enjoyment in the outing.

This break in the day and the timeless bonding ritual of margaritas and music broke through my surly wall and I found myself able to relax and ultimately enjoy what became a significant and pivotal day for our daughters.

I am grateful to this group of women who noticed that I needed them and then drew me out to play. Not once did anyone ask questions, scrutinize, or judge me. I was just me, hanging out with my friends, listening to their small talk with no pressure to do more than sit with them.

Never underestimate the power of friendship in its many forms.

GRATITUDE focuses UPON the PRESENT moment

WEEK 21

GRATITUDE FOCUSES UPON THE PRESENT MOMENT

EVERY MORNING, I FIND MYSELF STANDING AT MY KITCHEN SINK, FIRST THING IN THE MORNING, CUP OF TEA OR COFFEE IN HAND, STARING OUT THE WINDOW THAT OVERLOOKS MY LITTLE GARDEN.

I am grateful for this little piece of heaven. I have strategically placed a few feeders near the back fence amongst the roses. Many birds have discovered this stash of seeds; they eat every morning while I watch their simple feeding ritual.

I return to watch the birds whenever I feel anxious. This is a reset button of sorts for me. I cannot stay anxious during the "bird show." It is a sight to behold. They perch in my beautiful tree and hover near my kitchen window when the seeds rations are low.

This mindful, wakeful meditation is just what I need to remember to be fully present. Whatever I am doing is better when given my full attention. It reminds me to be grateful for the life that I am living.

Preparing meals, paying bills, cleaning bathrooms, and rushing off to work are tasks of daily life, made richer by cherishing the opportunity to do them at all. Gratitude for the life I am building, in all its minutiae, focuses upon the present moment.

🪷

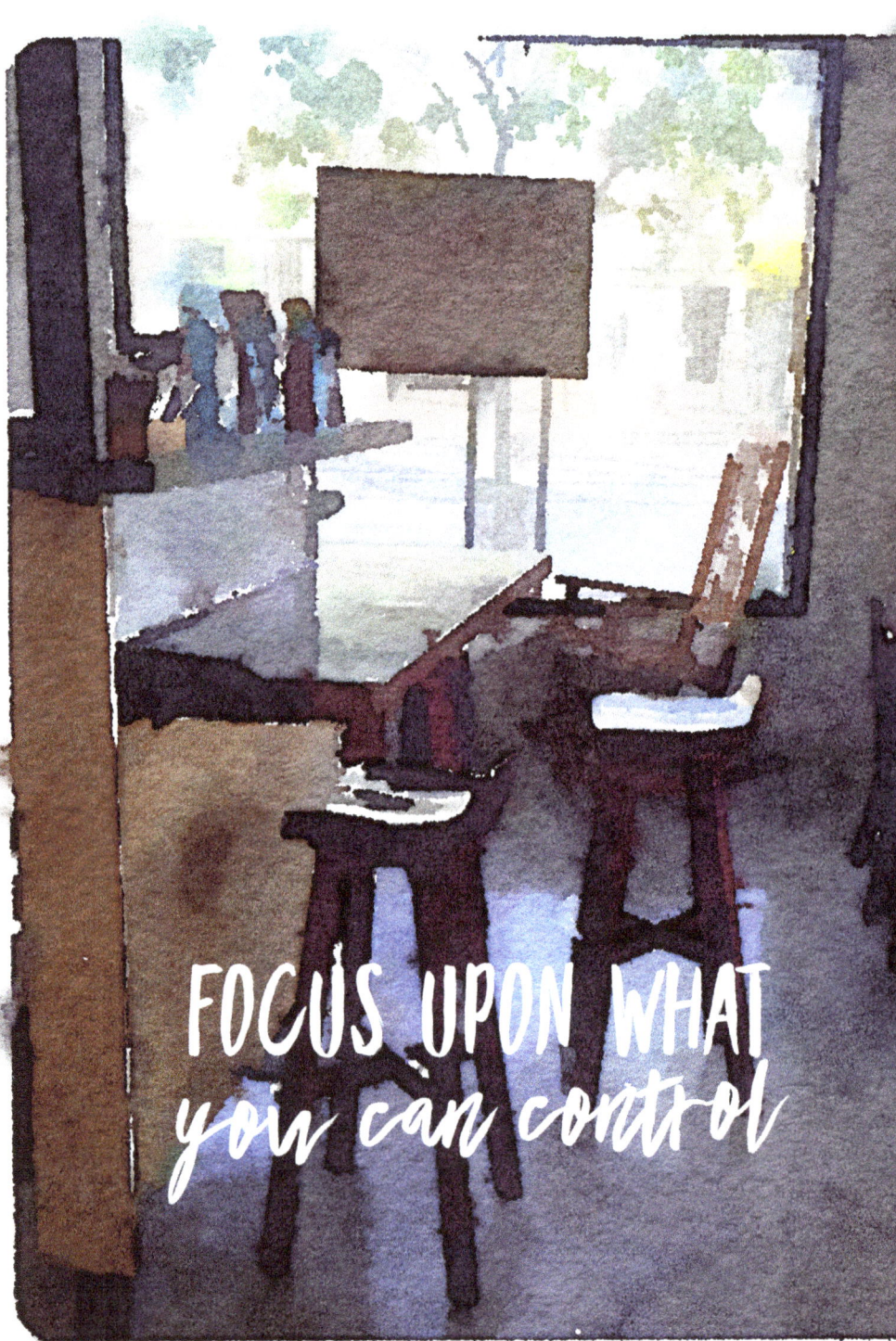

FOCUS UPON WHAT
you can control

FOCUS UPON WHAT YOU CAN CONTROL

My inability to maintain focus under times of stress and crisis felt demoralizing and debilitating. At first, I found it exhausting to make simple decisions and felt overwhelmed by life in general. Keeping it together in the beginning was just an act . . . me going through the motions. I started with simple, necessary activities like laundry and meal planning.

It may sound trite, but even planning a dinner menu for my children and me became a victory. It was also a sign of normalcy and comforting to all three of us. My kids would ask what I was fixing for dinner, and I wanted to have a delicious answer for them.

I have a new appreciation for the value of comfort food. It is as much about the context in which it became habitual as it is about how good it tastes. For us it was baked chicken, roasted potatoes, and fresh salads. It is still our go-to healthy, comforting meal. My ex-husband has called more than once to ask how I prepare my chicken. I have thought this ironic. He was the far better cook when we met. Truly! But I was paying attention when he prepared food. Since then I have learned a trick or two of my own.

Focusing upon what was within my control led me to dig deeper and to determine what was most important in each day and to let go of the rest. I approach each day with this two-fold question: "What is the best use of my time, and what is most important?" Sometimes the answer is not within my complete control, but when I focus upon the most important thing, and one thing at a time, there is usually time to find the answers to what I don't understand or the inspiration to seek an expert to help me.

As I took charge of what was within my control, I felt a sense of calm and peacefulness that had been missing. I was finding little pieces of myself again.

FOCUS ON *what is* MOST IMPORTANT

WEEK 23

FOCUS ON WHAT IS MOST IMPORTANT

I HAVE HEARD IT SAID THAT WE MAKE TIME FOR WHAT IS MOST IMPORTANT TO US. This may be true, but some days I become mired in the stuff of life that doesn't truly matter, and that doesn't lead me to the joy, compassion, and connection that I seek in my life.

On days that I found myself grieving my losses or stressing about the challenges of daily life, I found that checking in with my priorities helped me focus upon what was truly important to me.

When I do this, I find that my time, money, and energy are applied where they are truly most important to me. And I feel calmer and more confident about my choices.

I use a planner. I make notes, set goals, love to check off what I have completed, *and* I don't mind moving a task to a later date when it is the best use of my time after a review of my priorities. I no longer see this as a failure to finish my to-do list. Instead, I see it as honoring what is most important to me.

I think we all understand how much better things look on paper than in reality. Sometimes we underestimate how long a task will take or don't allow for complications. On the days that I feel overwhelmed or am overscheduled, I look for what can be moved to another day or can simply be dropped from my to-do list. I also schedule time for *nothing,* which allows me to pause, rest, and relax.

Leaving space in my day for *nothing* gives me time to regroup and recharge. Giving myself permission and time to sit quietly is a compassionate gift and a powerful tool for my health and well-being.

At the end of the day, I clear my desk, review my plan for the next day, reset my priorities if need be, and acknowledge what has been good in my day.

GIVE TO OTHERS,
pay it forward

GIVE TO OTHERS, PAY IT FORWARD

At first, I wanted the world to stop long enough for me to catch my breath, as if this somehow respected the enormous change in my life. The loss and the grief I felt was real and painful.

I wallowed, had pity parties for one, stamped my feet, and was miserable. I lay awake at night with ice cream, watched movies at 3 a.m., and cried to my friends. But this eventually grew tiresome. And not just for them.

I was honestly ready for the world to turn again and to no longer revolve around me. This growing restlessness signaled that I was healing! It was about this time that I decided to write my first book. This book.

It occurred to me that if I had these feelings, and that if I anguished over what it all means, if I wasted time with self-judgment and remorse, and if I asked the unanswerable question, "Why me?" then perhaps other people did, too. Could my story help someone else? Could sharing my story be one way of paying it forward? I hope so.

So here I sit, admitting to you that I felt petty and angry, but grew tired of feeling mean-spirited. I didn't like myself in those moments. I felt the need to stay home and withdraw from others, but I eventually missed conversation and connection with the world.

It turns out that what I needed was to focus on someone else for a change. As I focused my energies on others, I discovered that my value as a person had not been lost. There are so many opportunities for me to pay it forward by connecting with other people with no expectations.

I found a cause that speaks to my heart and got involved. I said yes more often when colleagues needed help with scheduling. I reached out to people I hadn't seen for a while, and I searched for childhood friends and let them know what they have meant to me. I stopped waiting to be asked to social events and made the first gesture. I felt joy and contentment as I reconnected with the world around me.

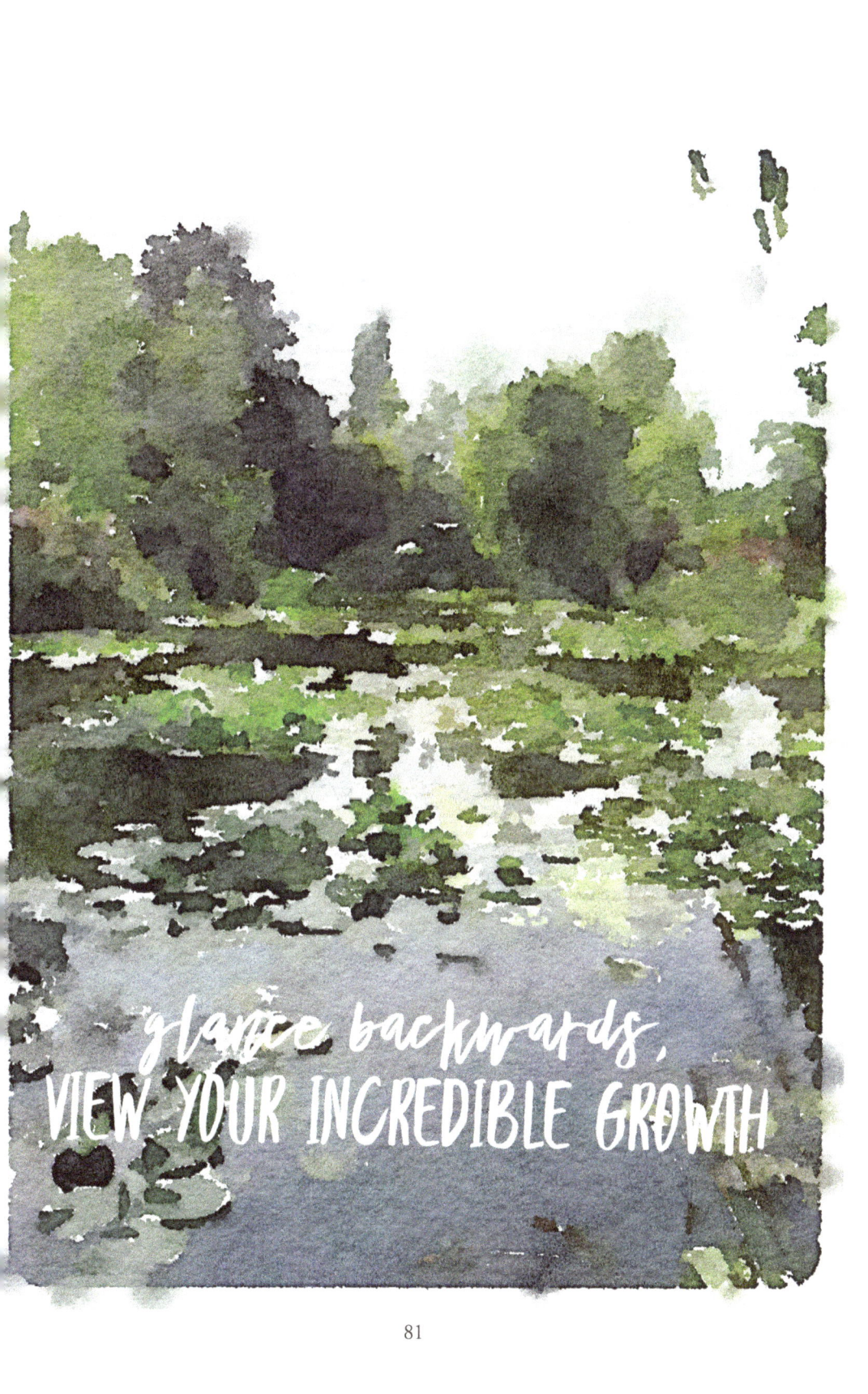

glance backwards,
VIEW YOUR INCREDIBLE GROWTH

WEEK 25

GLANCE BACKWARDS, VIEW YOUR INCREDIBLE GROWTH

THEY SAY, "HINDSIGHT IS 20/20." My hindsight gave me pause to admire, relish, and celebrate my incredible growth. On days that I felt stuck or slipped into the habit of harshly judging myself, it helped to remember what I was doing or feeling the previous year. The changes were much easier to see when looking back, and that inspired me to celebrate my progress.

Yet I was afraid that if I stopped feeling or thinking about what had transpired, it would negate my experience. The truth is, it's unhealthy to relive pain and trauma repeatedly.

Remember my fondness for films? I love television series as well and find comfort in re-watching familiar stories. An all-time favorite is *The West Wing*. One episode that stands out to me focused upon *Josh*, a character who had been seriously wounded and continued to relive the traumatic event leading to his injury.

As I was watching him work through his emotions surrounding the event, I realized that I had done the same thing to myself in my own way. I had allowed myself to repeatedly relive my feelings of shame, insignificance, and invisibility. I was repeatedly traumatizing myself every time I told my story to myself or someone else when I said he left me for a younger, prettier woman. Stopping this pattern was critical for my mental health and well-being.

Now when someone asks what led to our divorce, I no longer say "He left me for greener pastures and a younger cow," because honestly it was much more complicated than that, funny as that image is.

When I could retell my story without feeling as if it was happening in real time and could tell a kinder, gentler, less judgmental version, I knew I was making progress and was healing.

I was not dismissing the significance of what I had experienced. Glancing back for perspective is useful when the information strengthens what I know and believe to be true about marriage and relationships and adds perspective going forward. It doesn't limit me.

I am more than my past. I can expand and grow.

time
TO ACKNOWLEDGE,
accept, and release

WEEK 26

TIME TO ACKNOWLEDGE, ACCEPT, AND RELEASE

Letting go is kind. Owning only what is truly mine is imperative. Not easy.

One of my favorite magazines is *Oprah*, and I read it cover to cover every month. February 2015 posted an article written by Iyanla Vanzant, host of OWN's *Iyanla: Fix My Life*, and the author of *Peace From Broken Pieces*. Her important words rang true for me.

She answers the question of how to mend a broken heart by stating, "People can correct or heal only what they are ready to acknowledge, accept, and release."[6] Powerful words. Empowering words. At a time when I felt a loss of control and blamed others and the circumstances,

---

6 Iyanla Vanzant, "How to Mend a Broken Heart," *Oprah* Magazine, February 2015, http://www.oprah.com/inspiration/iyanla-vanzant-how-to-heal-a-broken-heart.

she reminded me that I do have choices, and it is up to me to take that responsibility for my own life and my own momentum.

Sounds simple, but there is more to it than deciding to let go and change my way of thinking. Taking responsibility has been one of the most difficult lessons for me and the most powerful. I have had the good fortune to find a trusted therapist who explained to me the neuroscience of stress and worked with me on the practical application of healthy change.

The neuroscience of stress has been explained to me in this way: There lies within each of us neural pathways that have been etched over time. Our default in times of stress is to return to the most deeply engrained of these. Knowing this, we could feel powerless and resist fighting something this established within our brains.

The good news is that we *can* etch new pathways. But it takes effort, dogged determination, repeated practice. It takes attending and acknowledging and actively releasing the negative, unhealthy, unproductive, destructive measures and stories that we use to replay past hurts and injuries. It takes deep breathing, and forgiveness. And it takes returning time and again to a state of peaceful calm.

I have a long-standing habit of filling in the blanks or making up stories when I don't have information. Stepping back, taking a deep breath, and letting the truth be the story, or letting myself be content with seeking more information before jumping to a conclusion, has resulted in less anxiety and more peacefulness in my daily life.

Each time that I recognize and acknowledge this pattern, accept my own limitations and flaws, and then release my negativity, I etch newer, more positive and healing pathways that will eventually become deeper and more entrenched in my brain. I believe this. This new, stronger pathway will become my new default, and resentment and hurt will no longer have power over me.

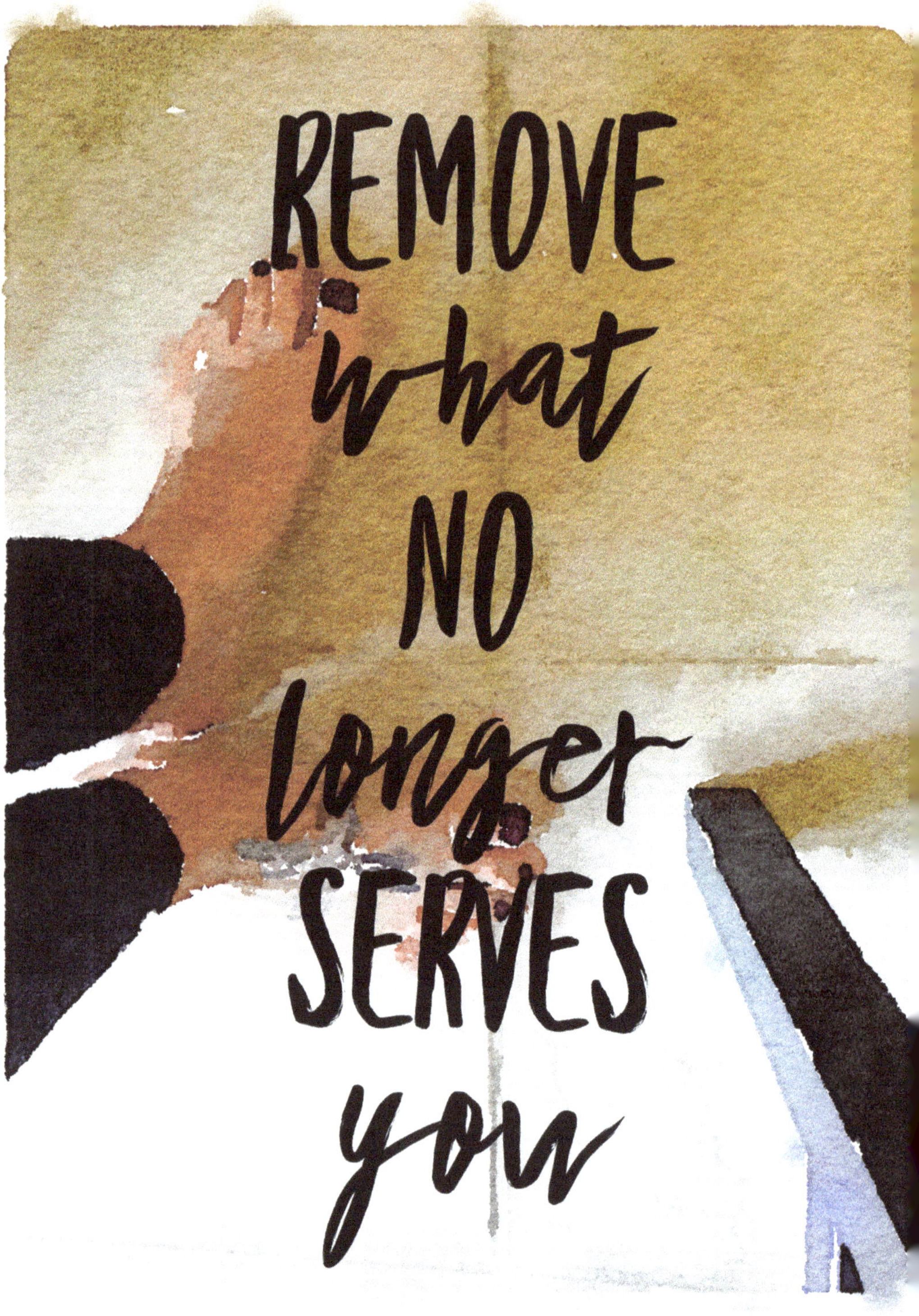
REMOVE
what
NO
longer
SERVES
you

WEEK 27

REMOVE WHAT NO LONGER SERVES YOU

To remove what no longer serves you requires that you acknowledge what is no longer working or serving your best interests. I'm referring to the clutter of life, the clutter that comes in both physical and emotional forms.

Acknowledging my emotional baggage, looking at my past with kinder eyes and with the knowledge that we each do our best at any given moment are important steps. There are wonderful books devoted to this idea. I found Brené Brown's work particularly relevant.

But what about the other "stuff"?

In the beginning, I felt so vulnerable and exposed as I shed the physical stuff of my married life. My attachment to things became clear to me.

I was asking myself to do what I ask my clients: to separate my memories from the physical stuff around me. And I didn't like it!

I lived in England and Wales the first three years of my marriage. During that time, I grew to appreciate antiques and collectibles and found a beautiful way to mix these treasures with the practical and the modern items of our daily life. And it suited us. I resented the task of separating treasure into his and hers. I was unprepared to let go of half. But removing his stuff and sharing half of what we had collected also removed some of the triggers that prevented me from growing forward. And this has been a good thing. I have enough, and what remains evokes happy memories.

The relinquished items are no longer missed. Letting go of them left empty spaces that no longer feel awkward to me. I find that I pause before filling them with something else. These spaces have become a reminder of what is yet to come into my life, and I am deliberate in my choices.

Until recently, I allowed myself to keep copies of emails and notes, exchanges between my ex-spouse and the *other woman*. They were somehow a final punishment, a reminder that I had failed in my marriage, like a bad report card or an F on a term paper that proved that I was a fraud and that my 8th grade teacher was correct in her assessment of my lack of ability.

When I let go of this need to punish and judge myself, I found I no longer needed the physical evidence of his betrayal, and the shredding was a simple task.

As I sorted and relinquished things from the house and garage to my ex-husband, I was also left with stuff that no longer served the kids and me in our current life. Together we agreed to find better homes for many items and became healthier for it.

I *peeled another layer of the onion (letting go a layer at a time)* when I prepared to sell my house and move. This letting-go stirred memories and emotions for me, but keeping too much no longer serves me well. Keeping just what I need, use, and love is my sweet spot!

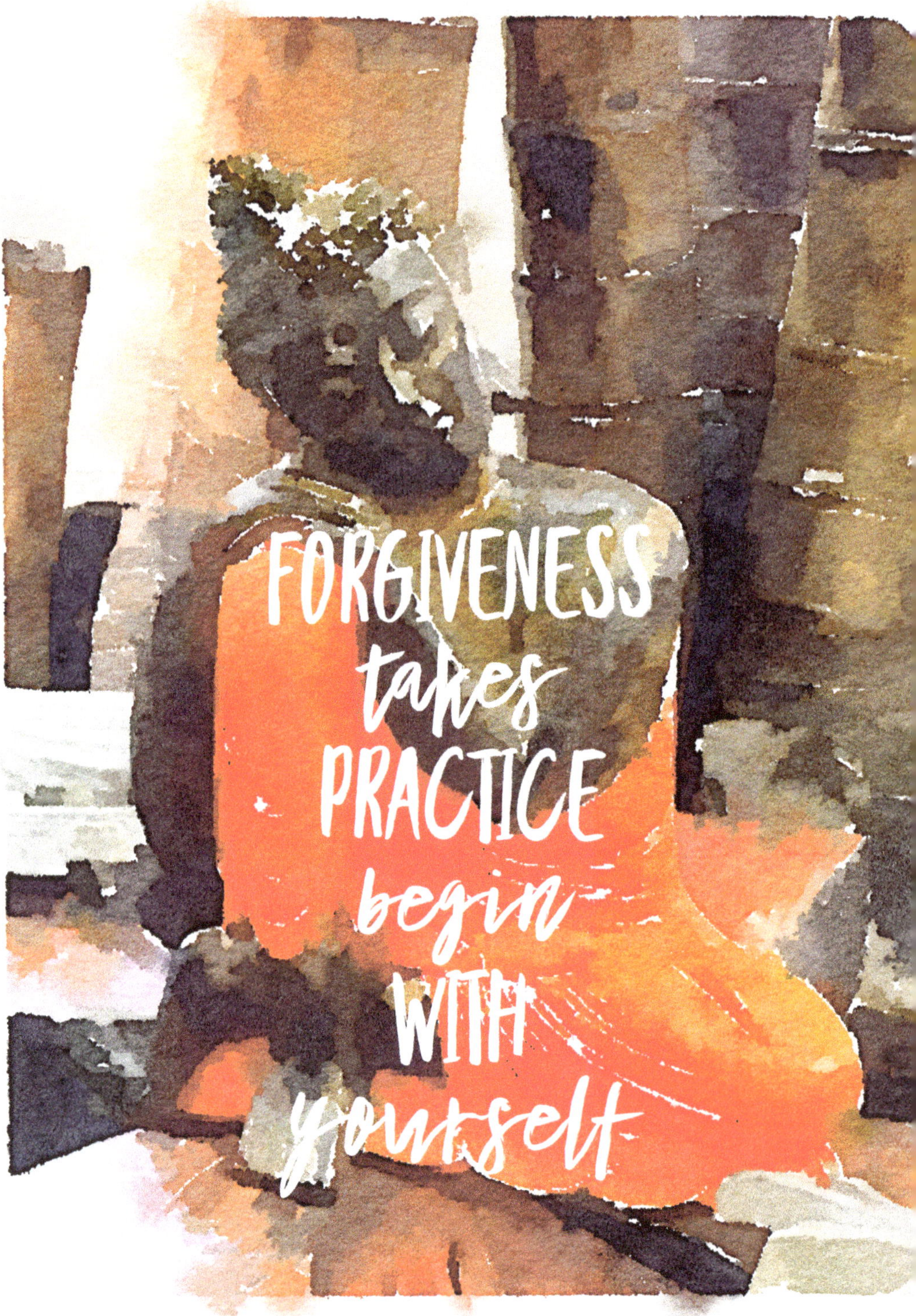
FORGIVENESS
takes
PRACTICE
begin
WITH
yourself

WEEK 28

FORGIVENESS TAKES PRACTICE, BEGIN WITH YOURSELF

Letting go of my constant self-judgment and emotional baggage took longer than the removal of the physical stuff of my marriage. Accepting that I had contributed to our miscommunications and acknowledging that my expectations for a relationship were flawed meant admitting that I had erred and was partly to blame for the end of our marriage. This knowing was painful.

I expressed anger at God for allowing pain to touch my children and me. And I blamed myself. It's difficult to let go of a lifetime of Catholic guilt and shame.

I believed that this failure to maintain a thriving relationship was ultimately my fault. Words such as "We get what we deserve" or "We sleep in the bed we make" nagged at me and fueled this belief that I was somehow to blame.

For a while, God didn't exist for me, at least not in the father-figure-doling-out-advice-with-tough-love-and-a-firm-hand way. A good father does not choose to feed some of his children and not others. We need only turn on the TV to see the catastrophic challenges in the world. In these moments, I feel small and humbled.

It took a year to truly release my anger, to embrace a universal collective energy, and to allow my own spiritual self to flourish again. And that included forgiveness, the cornerstone of my moving forward.

If I assume that people always do the best that they can, then I *must* extend this same courtesy to myself. My best may not always have stellar results, but it is what is possible at any given moment. I understand that I made decisions and choices based upon who I was and my life experience to that point, as did he. Forgiving *him* took longer, but became easier with practice.

I changed as I traversed the grieving process and survived my losses. This kinder perspective required a forgiving heart.

❧

close
DOORS,
open
WINDOWS,
stay
OPTIMISTIC

CLOSE DOORS, OPEN WINDOWS, STAY OPTIMISTIC

Forgiving does not equal forgetting. I remind myself of this when I struggle with the shifting dynamics of my family. Because we share two children, we need to speak with each other on a regular basis and there are shared holiday events to manage. The way things *were* is a closed door.

Yet there have been moments that I mistakenly gave words or gestures unintended meanings and felt a glimmer of hope that maybe our relationship could be salvaged after all. I feel vulnerable for admitting this here, but I suspect I am not alone in this. Letting go of my longing for what can never be between us is a door that has finally shut.

It took a lot of soul searching, but what I am clear on is the need to be with someone who truly values me and wants me in his life. I have yet to meet him, but I believe he exists. I am optimistic that living the life that suits me will bring new people into my life. But there is no rush. My eyes and my heart are open windows.

In the meantime, I have learned to speak more kindly and collaboratively with the father of my children. Harsh words can never be taken back. I know this only too well. So I am learning patience and practicing this when I speak with him. We both made assumptions based upon our past histories. This is no longer useful, and it certainly doesn't help us to move forward healthfully.

Being clear when we speak to each other and truly listening to each other takes energy, a real commitment to leaving hurtful memories in the past, and an optimistic belief that we are both doing the best we can. I am practicing what I didn't do well in my marriage.

I am optimistic that my future relationships will be better because of the lessons I am learning now. And I am hopeful that the pain that my children have felt throughout this process will be replaced with optimism for their own futures.

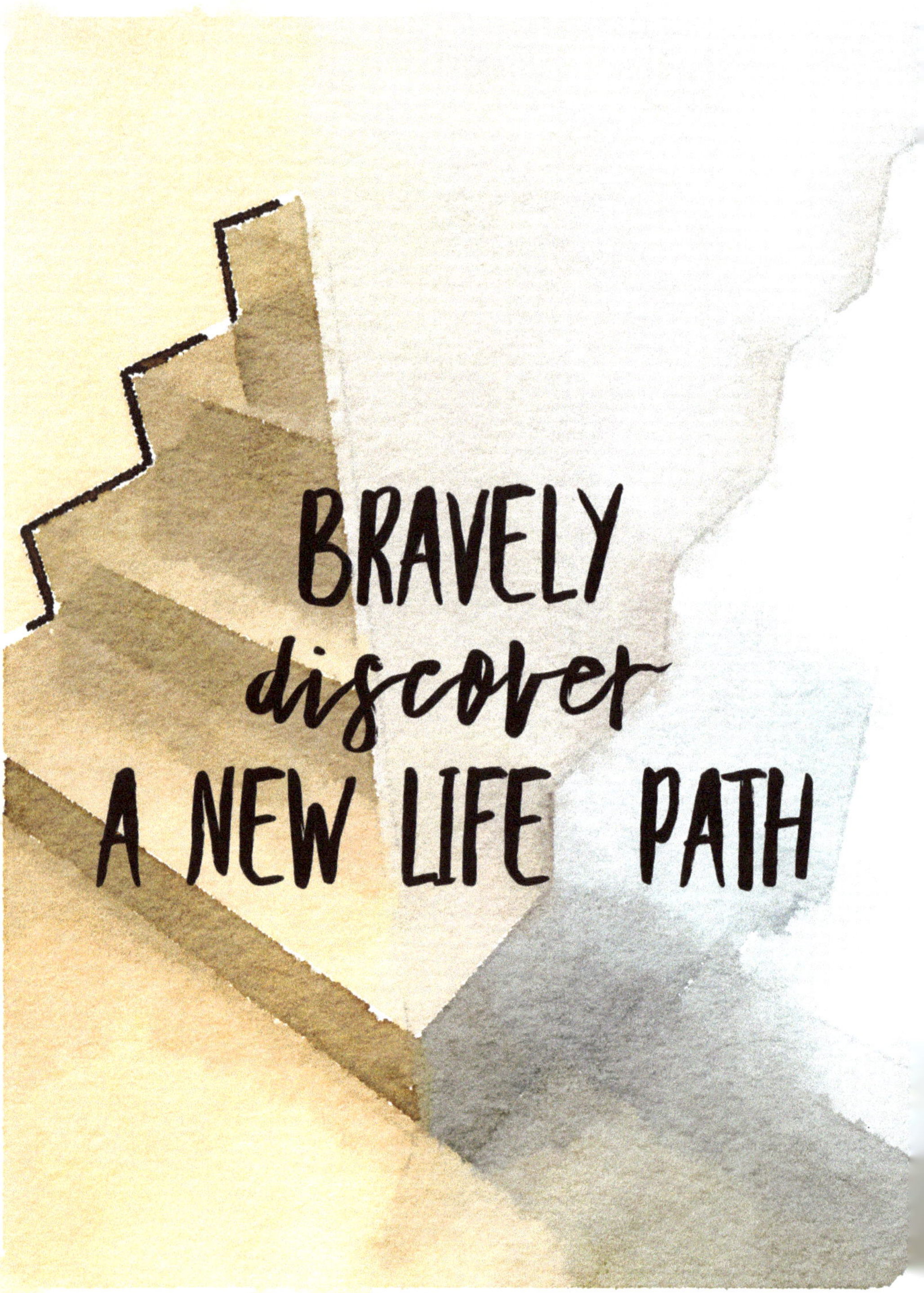
BRAVELY
discover
A NEW LIFE PATH

WEEK 30

BRAVELY DISCOVER A NEW LIFE PATH

I *ALWAYS* KNEW I WANTED TO BE A MOM. I clearly remember falling in love with the idea the year that my youngest sister was born. I was eight years old at the time. As I grew older, my desire to be a mother included the desire to find a life partner, to be married, and to share family life.

I was a stay-at-home mom, a decision that made sense given our frequent moves with the Navy. Staying home allowed me to be available to my family without work conflicts.

I worked part-time jobs off and on over the course of my marriage, but my jobs always took a back seat to the needs of my family. I found volunteering in the schools and teaching art to be a better use of my time and talents, and a better fit for my changeable schedule and needs. I was fully committed to this participation.

Marriage and family was the life I gladly poured myself into, body and soul. I have no regrets marrying the man that I loved. Our life together was blessed in many ways.

Our children are my greatest blessings and the most unselfish part of me. They are adults now who need less and less from me. Emptying my nest while my marriage dissolved was cruel timing. Yet I am proud to watch them take steps toward their independence.

The bravest thing that I have done through this whole process is to face my loneliness and aloneness head-on, blinders off, and then pave a new life path forward. When I realized that my old career was no longer a good fit, I searched my soul and decided to start my own business, choosing to create a service where my passions meet my skills and where I can be in service to others. I love what I do. The flexibility that it affords me is the icing on the cake!

As my business grows and I make efforts to reconnect with friends, I find my loneliness has dissipated. Loneliness has been replaced with an appreciation for the pauses in my day that solitary life affords me. I make space and energy for new relationships and find joy in my daily life.

My new path is becoming more familiar and more comfortable as time passes.

ALWAYS FALL
asleep
WITH A DREAM

ALWAYS FALL ASLEEP WITH A DREAM

FRAMED AND HANGING NEXT TO MY BED IS A SIMPLE BLACK-AND-WHITE MESSAGE TO MYSELF. It reads: *Always Fall Asleep With A Dream And Wake With A Purpose.* As I slip into bed, I see this and ask myself the same question night after night, "How *do* I want my life to look and feel and be?"

I am a visual person, and I find this visible reminder to set an intention comforting. In my aloneness, I have become my own cheerleader and coach of sorts. I read thought-provoking books, inspiring books, books that teach and encourage the growth that I seek personally. And I do my best learning and my best thinking in the solitude of my home.

I fall asleep thinking about something positive, which leads to deeper, more restful sleep; and equally important to me was this discovery. One night while having a disturbing dream, I remember saying no to the ending. I rewound the story while I slept; yet I was aware that I was doing so. That night I changed the ending. This elicited a tremendous sense of empowerment, and the sensation lingered as I awoke.

Imagine that! I no longer fear my dream state, nor do I worry about the hidden meanings of my dreams.

They say we problem-solve in our sleep. If the last question and thoughts in my head as I fall asleep inspire me to move in the direction of my heart, then asking myself the questions that set my life's course makes perfect sense to me: "How *do* I want my life to look, and feel, and be?" The knowledge that I can change the ending of my dreams gave me confidence that I can also change the course of my life.

Most days I rise energized and ready to face my day, often with a new idea or solution in hand. And at the end of the day, I ask the same question again and fall asleep to dream peacefully.

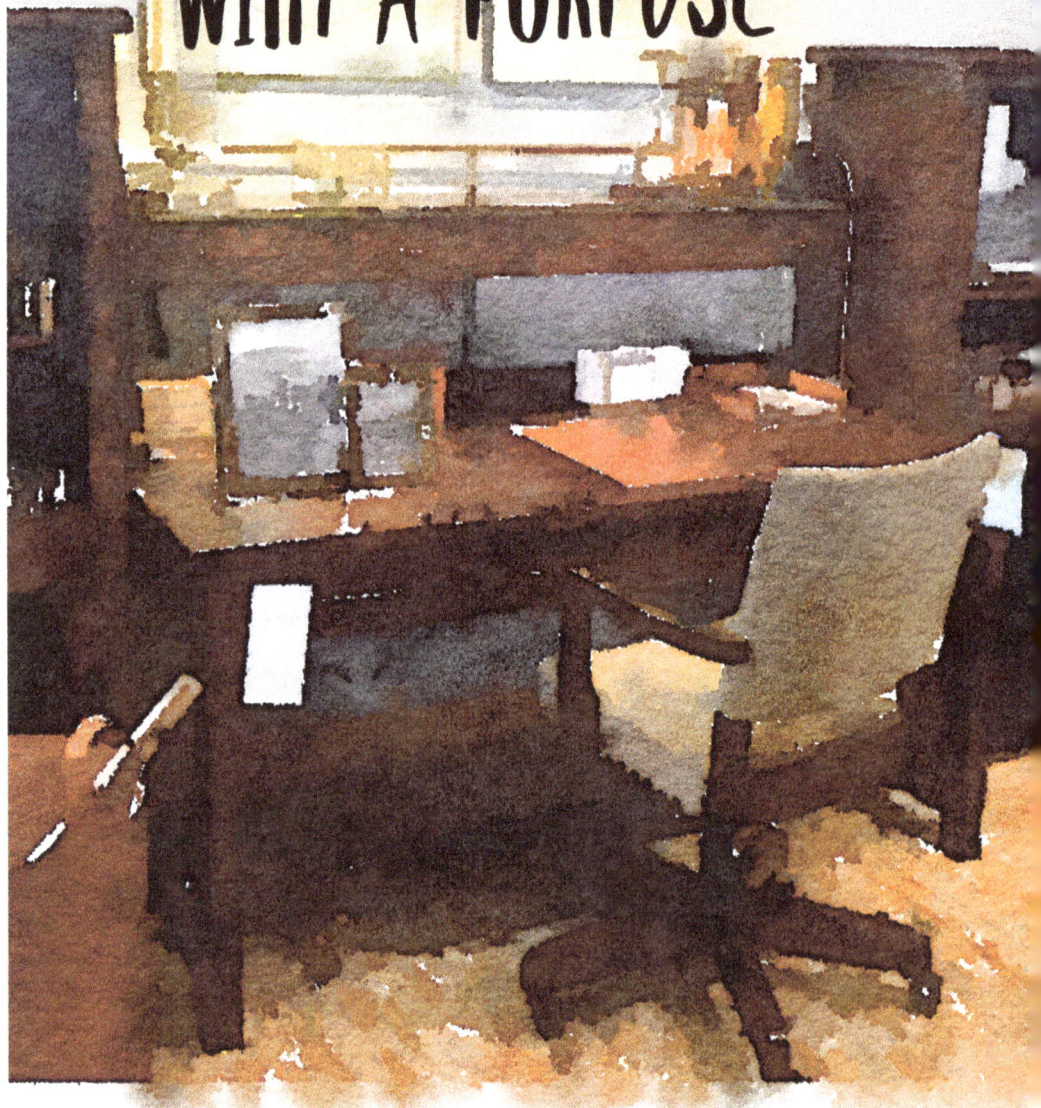

always wake up
WITH A PURPOSE

ALWAYS WAKE UP WITH A PURPOSE

WHAT I DESIRE UPON WAKING IS AN ENERGY AND SENSE OF PURPOSE AND DIRECTION FOR MY DAY. Having fallen asleep dreaming of my new life, I begin my day thinking about the steps that will take me where I want to go.

As an organizer, I practice what I encourage others to do. I use a daily planner. One of the last things I do before sleeping is glance at the next day's agenda and make any adjustments that seem necessary.

My daily activities include steps that focus upon family life, my personal growth, my health, home and garden, finances, business development, and future travel. Yes! I am always planning my next adventure. Currently, I have my heart set upon a trip to Italy, and my next drive up the coast to visit family. I have audio recordings to study Italian over the next year and am carving out a week for my road trip this summer. Both plans bring a smile to my face.

I find that my contentment and fulfillment, even while working on the minutiae of life, are richer because I know the choices I make are leading me in the direction of my choosing. And I am enjoying the journey of it all.

What I choose is to be fully engaged and mindful in my day. I know and believe that today is important. If I am doing what fulfills me, what moves me toward my heart's desire for connection, compassion, and creativity, then my life has meaning.

Knowing where I am going is important, but I can't become so focused upon the end or goal that I forget to enjoy the messy, complicated, beautiful present that I am living right now. I know I will glance back at the early days and celebrate how much I have grown through purposeful, mindful, one-step-at-a-time living.

find the
HEART
of what
MATTERS

WEEK 33

FIND THE HEART OF WHAT MATTERS

FINDING THE HEART OF WHAT MATTERS BEGAN AND REMAINS A FOUNDATION FOR MY BUSINESS. Over time this same mantra has become pivotal in my personal life as well. After all, for me, everything is connected. "The heart of what matters" is as individual as we are. It represents the driving force in our lives— what we wish and hope for, what makes us tick, the values at our very core.

Finding less stress and more joy by honoring what I want most from life is my ultimate goal. It requires introspection and honesty. But this epiphany did not come easily. It took many hours, and months, of self-reflection, study, review of inspirational books, and cognitive behavior therapy, lots of it! My goals and purpose shifted when my marriage ended. What lies at the core of who I am and how I live my life did not. It just took a while to remember.

There is a book by Suzanne Evans called *The Way You Do Anything Is The Way You Do Everything.*[7] I saw it while perusing books in an airport

---

7   Suzanne Evans, *The Way You Do Anything Is the Way You Do Everything* (Hoboken, NJ: J. Wiley & Sons, 2014).

bookstore and found the title intriguing. Can you guess what I read on my flight?!

At the end of the day, if how I do anything is how I do everything, then I had best know where I stand, know my deepest convictions, and my core values.

For me, the three words that I hold dear and that drive me personally and professionally are connection, compassion, and creativity. These are at the heart of who I am, what I do, and how I frame my life.

Knowing this about myself, and leading from this place has made decision-making and prioritization clearer for me because I am clear about the heart of what matters most to me.

look and Plan
A NEW NORMAL

LOOK AND PLAN A NEW NORMAL

Find a new normal is a borrowed idea. I don't remember where I first heard it because I heard it many times from different sources. But these words, "find a new normal," gave me a sense of hopefulness and of control over my own destiny.

I certainly didn't expect to be single after 25 years of marriage. But here I am starting over, setting a course toward a contented, joyful future. I feel grateful that the decision to sell our family home and to establish my nest somewhere new is a choice that I can make. I feel grateful that I have enough to rebuild my life and that I have the freedom to make choices that suit me. Letting go of what no longer fit made room for my new life and my new normal.

How many times did I start to do something in the same way that I had in my married life, only to remember that I no longer needed to consider my spouse's likes and dislikes, needs and wants? This was disarming at first, but as time moved on, I learned to love and appreciate this freedom to explore *my* purchases, *my* home, and *my* personal time in new and fresh ways!

I find I am adding more color to my home and my wardrobe. I no longer want to blend in or disappear, though I do still appreciate my solitude. I am repurposing my favorite things in new and creative ways. And my schedule is mine to plan as I see fit.

If there is something you have always wanted to do or try, there is no time like the present to jump in and learn a new skill, find a new hobby, eat when you are hungry, watch a movie just for you, and read that stack of books that has been patiently waiting for you.

At first it felt awkward, and the silences and quiet were deafening and too large to fill. Then one day, without even noticing the shift, I realized I enjoy the pauses in the day, and even look forward to the silence, and the new normal in my routine.

TIME to REDISCOVER what YOU love

TIME TO REDISCOVER WHAT YOU LOVE

MAKING TIME TO DISCOVER WHAT YOU LOVE IS PART OF HEALTHY LIVING AND A HEALTHY FUTURE. It feeds you, body and soul, and requires active thought and planning.

After years of having a ready-made partner, I found myself entering the social world as a single woman. I had always wanted to learn ballroom or swing dancing, and I thought social dancing would be a good outlet for me. Truthfully, I felt awkward, and it took every ounce of courage to just set foot through the door.

I attended classes almost every week and braved a sea of strangers' faces, waiting like a wallflower for someone to ask me to dance or even more awkwardly making the gesture first. I did this for the better part of a year, attending classes and staying afterward to practice. My son even joined me on occasion. It didn't end up being the right fit for me socially, but what I discovered was that I really love exercising to music in any form.

And then I discovered ballet-inspired barre exercise classes. I found such a connection with the music and movement, and yes, the active mindfulness of it. It has become a favorite way to decrease my stress. I also know that when the day comes that this no longer suits me, I will be okay moving on to something else.

How long has it been since you truly explored the question, "What do I want?" Finding the answer takes practice and perseverance. But with practice, it becomes a habit. Discovering what I truly love has been yet another layer of self-discovery.

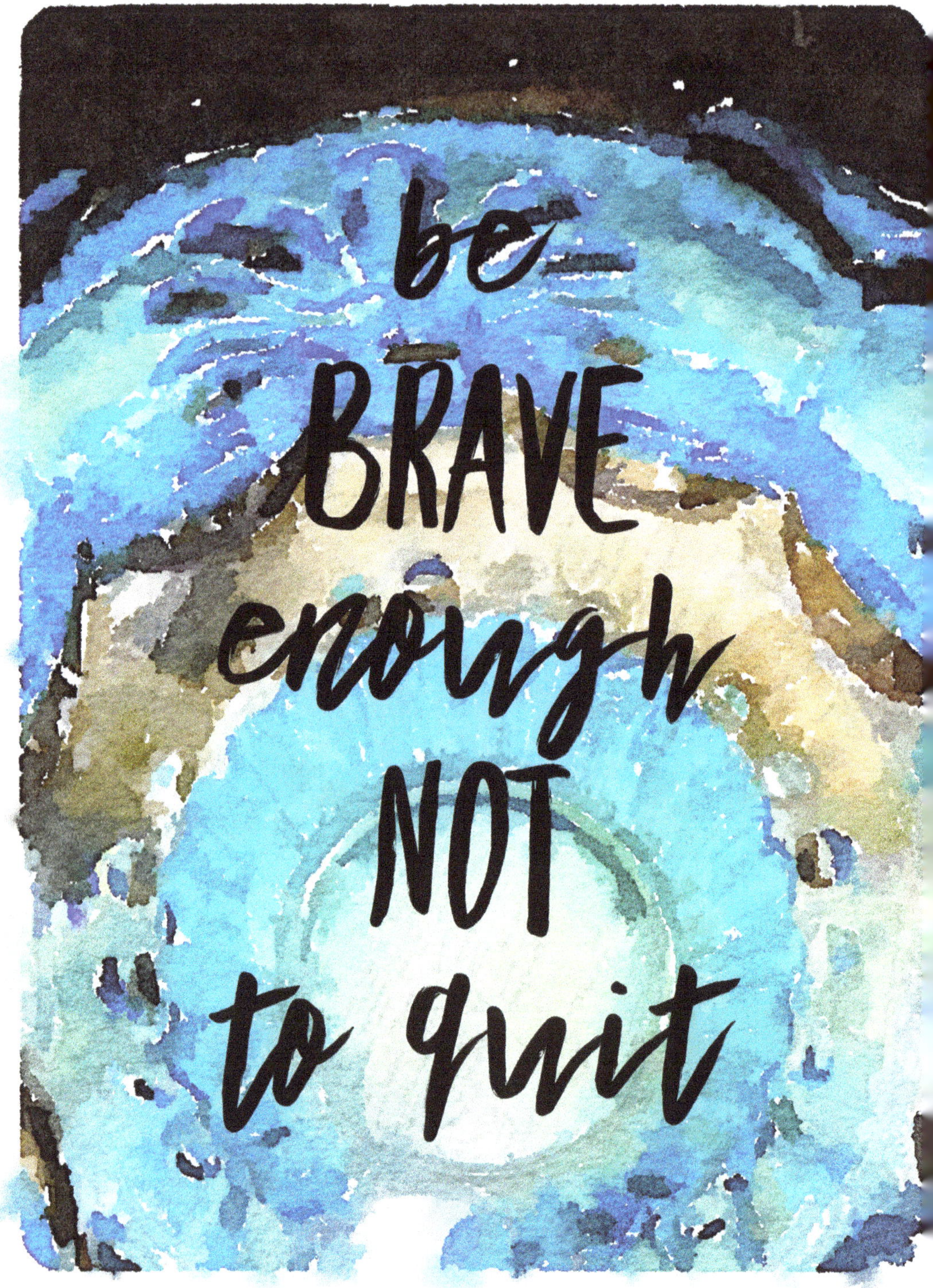
be
BRAVE
enough
NOT
to quit

BE BRAVE ENOUGH NOT TO QUIT

EVERY DAY I WEAR A RING WHICH BEARS THE INSCRIPTION: "BE BRAVE ENOUGH NOT TO QUIT."[8]

As you might imagine, this holds many layers of meaning for me. And yes, for a brief moment, in the very beginning, I wondered if my family would be better off without me. I knew deep in my heart that the answer to this was and is no, and I have never looked back or doubted this since then. My lifework is still in progress.

Being brave for my children was my first step. But the true breakthrough was when I chose to be happy for myself as well.

Today I wear the ring to remind me that I *am* strong, that I *am* focused, and that when I am clear about what is important to me, I feel happy. And I wear it to remember to begin with the end in mind.

8　"Be brave enough not to quit," ring with inscription designed and made by Delias Thomson, Atlanta, GA. Found on the Etsy website.

When I met my husband, I was working as a pediatric ICU nurse. In our first eight years of marriage, my husband's job with the military necessitated seven moves. I continued to work as a nurse until our first child was born, at which point we decided that it was best for our family that I stay home.

After our divorce, I attempted to reenter the nursing profession, but found that I no longer fit there. Too much has changed. *I* have changed. So I began a business utilizing the knowledge and skills that I have strengthened as a mother, as a volunteer, and those remembered from my years as a nurse. I have added my passions for creative problem-solving and organization, and found my purpose.

I also accepted a part-time job in retail. It added stability to my life as my business developed, and it gave me confidence in my worth at a time when my confidence was floundering.

I feel useful, valuable, and needed. And, yes, when there is a whirlwind of activity some weeks and an open calendar the next, having your own business can feel a little bit scary. Staying the course and being brave enough not to quit has become my mantra. My business is blossoming as I write this, but I know that there will be lulls and I will be brave enough to ride them out.

I know many who read this are working more than one job to make ends meet. I applaud and salute you. Be brave enough not to quit on yourself. Know where you are going and keep your eye on the goal as you navigate your life—messy bits and all.

look forward to
PAVE YOUR FUTURE

LOOK FORWARD TO PAVE YOUR FUTURE

So here I sit, aware of the importance of having some sort of written plan for myself. It is not written in stone and it's certainly open to discussion and change as I see fit. But planning is the first step toward making what I dream about a reality.

It is my New Year's Day tradition to begin with a list of everything that springs to my mind. It holds my ideas and dreams, and wishes for my future. Everything from adding a Meyer lemon tree to my balcony patio to planning a trip to Italy to scheduling my next dentist appointment is on this list. How I want my life to look and feel is also on this freestyle list.

Then the list gets broken down into manageable pieces and added to my project pages, and then to calendar pages. Although ideas and items may be removed or shift to new time slots as my priorities and budget change, planning gives me a structure and foundation for decision-making regarding my future.

And, yes, *being open to love* is on my list.

On a recent trip to New York City, I watched a beautiful movie production of Jane Austen's *Mansfield Park*. There is a scene where the protagonist in her heartbroken anguish exclaims her belief that "marriage is a maneuvering business."

Such harsh words spoken by this disillusioned woman. As time goes by, she becomes more confident in her ability to honor what she needs to be truly happy, and although tempted, does not compromise her values.

I realize now that I no longer view the possibility of finding love as ridiculous or something to be scorned. That said, I *do* have both eyes open. And, although I am in no rush, I *am* paving a future that makes room for love in my life alongside planting my lemon tree and all that sits on my list.

❧

Practice
KINDNESS
until
IT FEELS
natural

PRACTICE KINDNESS UNTIL IT FEELS NATURAL

It takes practice to behave kindly when you feel angry or disheartened. At least, I found this to be true for me. Responding to what sounded like stupid, insensitive, or prying questions required kindness. I had many opportunities to practice, and yes, it did become easier.

I will never forget being asked, "Have you had your younger man yet?" Oh, and, "Is this your post-divorce tattoo?"

I wasn't brave enough to give a sassy answer at the time, although surely my dumbfounded facial expression sent a clear message. I kindly laughed and said, "I was married to a younger man (okay, he was six months younger than me), and my hummingbird tattoo is a Native American talisman chosen thoughtfully to remind me to find joy and to celebrate life!"

People ask odd questions especially when they are at a loss for words, and I dig deeply to remember that the only point of view another person has is their own. This allows me to keep a sense of humor, to view statements less personally, and to show kindness to them and to myself when judgmental queries arise.

Despite countless hours of movie viewing and the example set by women with moxie and gumption, I do not think quickly on my feet. No easy elevator-pitch repertoire for me! My *after-wit,* however, is remarkably witty. I do not regret responding with kindness; however, I retold the story with this colorful embellishment, "What the fuck?! No one told me there was a checklist!"

Kindness and self-compassion became natural with time and practice. I felt less guilty listening to my heart, honoring what I needed, in my own time and in my own way. And I felt kinder toward others when their attempts to offer comfort or advice missed the mark. I learned to accept their words for the kindness that motivated them.

CELEBRATE YOUR VICTORIES
large and small

CELEBRATE YOUR VICTORIES, LARGE AND SMALL

THE DAY THAT I LOOKED TO MYSELF FIRST FOR THE ANSWERS TO A COMPUTER CHALLENGE WAS A SMALL VICTORY! This may not be a big deal to some people, but for me it was a milestone worth acknowledging.

For most of 25 years, I had looked to my spouse for tech support, knowing that he had more expertise and a greater interest in mastering the rapidly evolving world of technology than I did. Looking back, I realize that I handicapped myself by allowing someone else to do for me what I could do for myself.

I didn't believe that I could understand what I needed to know, and it was easier to let him fix the problems as they arose than to ask him to teach me. A pattern evolved early in our relationship. And, even after our separation, I would call to ask for his help with computer issues.

Before we met, I worked in a pediatric intensive care unit where technology was challenging and misuse could have life-threatening results. I used the technology well there. Why I ever let myself think I couldn't troubleshoot a computer, I don't know. But that all changed the morning I opened my computer to read emails and found that all my files were corrupted. I mean *all* of them.

I realized later that I hadn't once thought to call him first for advice. I managed the problem myself with the aid of experts who taught me what I didn't know. But I didn't call him. I had such a feeling of pride and accomplishment.

I know that I am going to be okay no matter what my future brings. With this simple action, I had remembered to trust myself and to appreciate my own problem-solving skills.

❧

utilize your resources,
STRENGTHEN YOUR INDEPENDENCE

UTILIZE YOUR RESOURCES, STRENGTHEN YOUR INDEPENDENCE

ONCE I BECAME BRAVE ENOUGH TO BE HONEST ABOUT MY FEELINGS, I FOUND THE RESOURCES TO HELP ME BUILD MY COURAGE AND STRENGTH. I did not have to grieve alone or figure everything out by myself. Opening up to close friends and my therapist felt safer over time and gave me new language and new strategies for strengthening my independence and rebuilding my confidence.

Once I became open and vocal about what I was experiencing, the floodgates opened. It was such a relief to lean upon someone else a little and to draw strength after feeling so lost and so diminished.

There are many resources available, whether it's counseling, financial planning, or a good masseuse. Just be sure to ask people you trust for the recommendations. When the same names appear repeatedly and from unrelated sources, you know you are in the right ballpark.

Also, if I have learned nothing else, I have learned that the decision of who to include in my life is *my* choice. I am remembering to trust my gut. If I feel uncertain about who I am inviting into my inner circle and experience a nagging feeling in my gut, I use caution. Never again do I need to lose sight of my needs or what is important to me.

I remember meeting a woman in a dance class who made it clear that she preferred her single existence and had no shame or embarrassment about it. I realized in that moment that I was ashamed of my failure to remain married. In my mind, it meant that I was unlovable.

No doubt I needed to reframe my view of myself. I wondered if I embraced the idea of enjoying all that being single afforded me, would I also feel less shame at being discarded and instead be grateful for the new opportunities in my life?

My new definition of myself became empowering and positive: I am a strong, capable, independent woman with adult children. I decide what is important to me, who I share my time with, and who I include in my circle of trust.

TIME TO
discover
WHAT
you
NEED

TIME TO DECIDE WHAT YOU NEED

We had 25 years of stuff and memories in our house, and it all needed to be divided and sorted. He left, saying he didn't want anything. I knew him well enough to know that his words came from a place of guilt and remorse, not truth. I could have just taken him at his word and kept everything, but I didn't.

A part of me wanted to pile his belongings on the front lawn and leave him a note. But that wouldn't have been true to my core values. I couldn't end things that way. I could, and did, hurl harsh words at him, but not the *stuff* that represented our lifetime together.

I thoughtfully sorted, packed, and labeled his belongings, and let him know when they were ready. His participation in this process was minimal, for which I am grateful. It gave me a sense of control in a confusing and sad time in my life. Honestly, the things he treasured were constant reminders of what I had lost; and as they left the house, I felt more and more at peace.

While my children's rooms remained unchanged, I needed the communal rooms to feel fresh and to represent my kids and me in this place in time; and so I began the process of repainting, moving furniture around, and saving money for a few pieces to replace what had exited with my ex-husband.

Family photos and special mementos from the first years of our marriage were the first things I removed. I needed to make visible changes if for no other reason than to show that I was accepting this monumental change in my life.

I was fortunate to remain in the home where I raised my kids until we all felt ready to let it go. When the day came to sell the family home, I was ready. I needed to come to that decision in my own time and will be forever grateful that I was afforded that gift of time. When the need to be independent and to have a fresh start somewhere else became stronger than the need to cling to the family home, I knew what I needed to do. We sold the house, and I left with a peaceful heart.

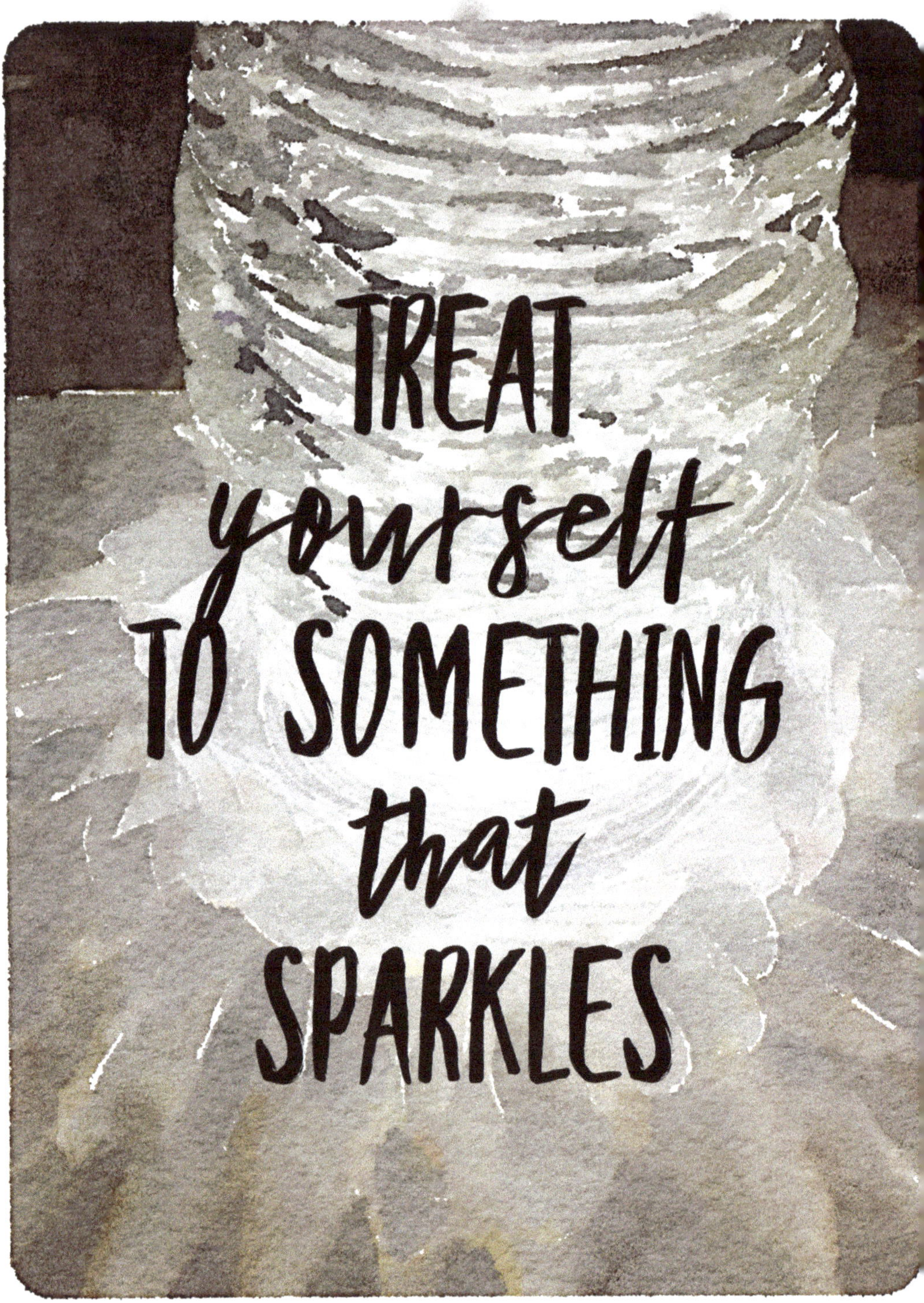
TREAT
yourself
TO SOMETHING
that
SPARKLES

WEEK 42

TREAT YOURSELF TO SOMETHING THAT SPARKLES

ARE YOU FAMILIAR WITH THE TERM "RETAIL THERAPY?" So am I. I admit to the urge to buy something shiny. I traded in my old car and leased another in my own name. This was the first time I had made this kind of purchase on my own in more than 25 years.

The car dealership had sold *us* cars in the past, and when I boldly asked for loan approval in the middle of mediation, the dealership took a leap of faith that I would consistently make monthly lease payments on my own. I am proud to say that I kept this commitment and appreciated my shiny, sparkling red car, the car that I bought all by myself. It helped me to establish credit in my name, and I will be forever grateful for the kindness of the people who had a little more faith in me than I had in myself.

Something shiny extended to keeping my kitchen spotless, highlighting my hair for the first time, and watching only happy, uplifting movies with witty, sparkling dialogue.

I indulge when and where I can to treat myself special. I eat off my favorite dishes, use my favorite glassware, and dress to suit myself. Yes, my go-to color is black; it has been for many years. But I make sure I accessorize with a favorite necklace or earrings to add a little sparkle and whimsy. Sometimes I overindulge, but the credit card bill is a sobering reminder to use caution. Retail therapy should be used judiciously.

My wedding bands and a few other sparkling pieces that I received during my marriage are tucked away for my daughter and son. I know they may want them some day. When that day comes, these beautiful treasures will be a reminder of the love that brought them into this world.

try
SOMETHING NEW,
laugh about it

WEEK 43

TRY SOMETHING NEW, LAUGH ABOUT IT

I AM HAPPY TO REPORT THAT ALTHOUGH IT WAS MISSING IN ACTION FOR QUITE A WHILE, MY SENSE OF HUMOR HAS RECOVERED AND IS IN FULL FORM. I choose to surround myself with uplifting, positive people as much of the time as possible.

A good friend of mine has chosen to search for companionship via the internet. I have not succumbed, despite her urging. But I do enjoy hearing her stories. If listening to her tales isn't a source of endless mirth, and food for self-reflection, I don't know what is. Her storytelling and recaps of the adventures of dating post-divorce are mortifying. I am not at liberty to share them here, but they rival any good, made-for-TV movie. Trust me!

Being out and about as a single woman after so many years feels new and awkward. But what harm could there be in smiling and noticing the people around me, right?

Alas! Just making eye contact with men my age has felt like a big, faulty misstep. While out for a coffee with my daughter, I smiled and greeted the man standing behind me. He was friendly, but then proceeded to follow my daughter to the counter. His eyes never left her backside.

I tried something new, and I laughed about it. But I think for now I will limit my harmless flirtations to times I am sans daughter. I'm sure it was a little creepy for her. After all, when you are 19, anyone over the age of 25 is ancient, if not practically dead.

I applaud my friend's courage in braving the internet dating world. As for me, I find being out in the world living my life, doing the things that I love to do is a better fit for me. I know that finding a man with a good sense of humor will happen in its own time. And it will most likely result in a story we can share and laugh about later.

❧

let
GOOD
enough
BE
good
ENOUGH

WEEK 44

LET GOOD ENOUGH BE GOOD ENOUGH

I AM LEARNING TO TRULY APPRECIATE THE VALUE OF LETTING GOOD ENOUGH BE GOOD ENOUGH. With divorce comes the reality of unrealized expectations and change. Lots of it!

Our first holiday season post-separation brought a myriad of questions that I was not ready to answer. What was once simple became complicated. Do my ex-husband, the kids, and I divide holidays between the two families? Do we trade off every other year? Do we have shared celebrations and meals? Will the kids be happy? Will I?

I have always loved the fall and the holidays, one on top of the next. It wouldn't be the same going forward. How could it be?!

From mid-October when we celebrate my son's birthday, until New Year's Day when we watch the Rose Parade or go to Julian for apple pie, a whirlwind of activities and celebrations ensued. Between those two dates were my daughter's birthday, my ex-husband's birthday, our anniversary, Thanksgiving, and Christmas. All were special to me. Now what?

To find normalcy and to ease into the transition of divorce, we agreed to travel together with our kids across the country to visit his family for that first post-divorce Thanksgiving. I had always looked forward to Thanksgiving with his family.

This gathering was historically a wonderful mix of cooking and eating and enjoying family time together. I did not want to give up this connection to the family that had become mine through marriage, nor did I want to miss being a part of the fun and memory-making going forward.

Yet, I felt trepidation. Although I wanted it to be magical, as it had always been, it was not. The reality was that I felt like an outsider. His family was warm and welcoming as always. But my ex-husband ignored me for three days. I was present but not completely included. I felt humiliated.

I decided that my new normal meant accepting that the holidays would look and feel different, messy, and awkward at times. I let go of my high expectations for constant, happy, carefree merriment. I am grateful for moments that feel calm and moments that bring joy. And what works for all of us will evolve over time.

For now, and going forward, that's good enough!

PRACTICE
self-compassion,
ACCEPT
your
LIMITATIONS

PRACTICE SELF-COMPASSION, ACCEPT YOUR LIMITATIONS

Brené Brown says, "The most dangerous stories we make up are the narratives that diminish our inherent worthiness. We must reclaim the truth about our lovability, divinity, and creativity."[9]

When I lose perspective, I put a tremendous amount of pressure on myself to be my version of perfect. When I fall short, I am disappointed. This unrealistic and unloving narrative reared its ugly head in the weeks after I moved to my new home.

Here I was amid a grand adventure—building my new life—yet the story I told myself was harsh. I said, "You should have all the answers. You should have no excess. You should not be struggling with your stuff. You are an organizer. You need to set a good example at all times."

---

9   Brené Brown, *Rising Strong* (New York: Random House, 2015), 82.

When I realized that I had given myself a different set of standards for moving and organizing my home than I have for others, I stopped short and reevaluated. I had forgotten to allow myself time and space to make decisions. I needed to show the same compassion to myself that I show others.

Slowing down to enjoy the process has made all the difference in this next step of rebuilding my life. My home looks beautiful, and mostly calm. Rather than fixate upon the messy parts, with boxes still to sort, photos to hang, and a garage with transitional stuff yet to be removed, I notice that my home is becoming the sanctuary I require.

There is no deadline. There is no one right or wrong way. I like this story much better. I am worthy of love and happiness.

kindness
SOMETIMES COMES
from unexpected places

WEEK 46

KINDNESS SOMETIMES COMES FROM UNEXPECTED PLACES

I VALUE AND APPRECIATE THE UNEXPECTED GIFT OF KINDNESS FROM COMPLETE STRANGERS. It has appeared in moments when I showed vulnerability. A smile from a bank teller or patience from someone on the other end of the phone can set the tone for my whole day.

I hope for and expect connection and kindness when amongst friends and family where I feel safe. I treasure and value this in my life.

But probably the most unexpected expression of kindness has come from my ex-husband. Because we share children, our lives are forever entangled. We decided early on during mediation that we would make every effort to be kind to each other.

In the early months of our separation and divorce, kindness didn't come easily. It often felt stilted and forced. But always in the back of my mind was how my actions and behaviors affected my children. Over time and with repeated practice, showing kindness became easier and felt more authentic.

And then we agreed to sell the house we still co-owned. This was the familiar-but-no-longer-comfortable space where we had raised our two children. I was ready to move on with my life. I *needed* to move on with my life.

The process of selling and packing moved at warp speed, and was accompanied by a myriad of emotions. I no longer found showing kindness easy. Kindness was replaced with feelings of irritation and impatience. Giving in to these emotions felt like a setback to me, albeit a normal response to the stress of moving.

Through it all, my ex-husband showed kindness and patience. I will be forever grateful for that. Despite his busy work life and his own feelings about selling the house, he rallied to sort and remove his belongings that still lingered in the garage, and to help with mine and the kids' things as well.

He showed surprise that I wasn't taking the ficus tree from the front porch. I didn't think much of it at the time. We had a ficus tree everywhere we had lived. These plants always represented health and healing to us. But this one had grown too large and heavy to move.

A few weeks later, he showed up at my new home with a miniature, bonsai-style ficus to welcome me to my new life. I was truly touched by his thoughtfulness and the *olive branch* that this tree represents.

My therapist once told me, "One is never really completely divorced." I now understand what he meant. There is history together that cannot be erased. It was not easy getting to this place of forgiveness and kindness, but it has allowed a healing I didn't think possible.

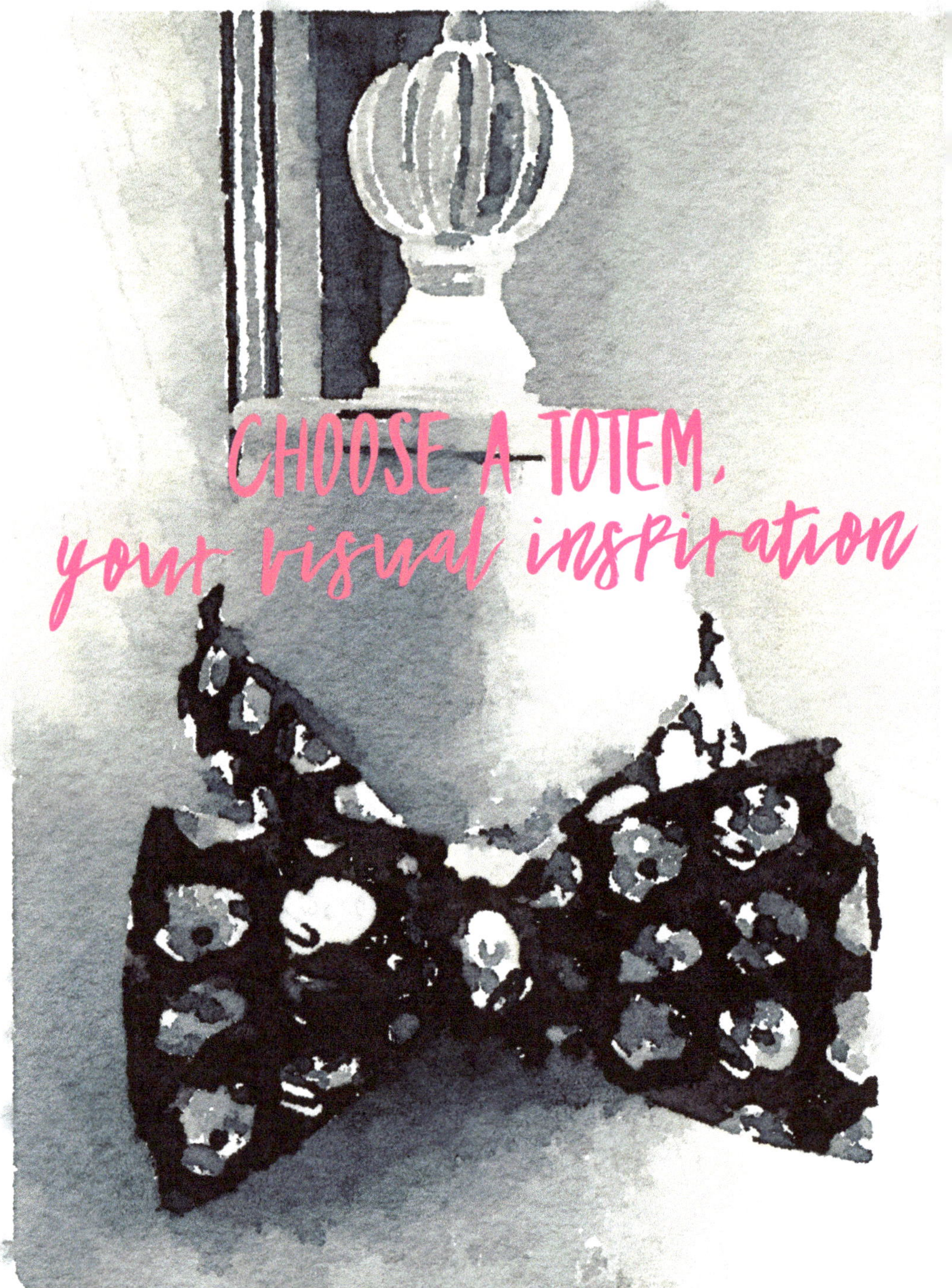
CHOOSE A TOTEM,
your visual inspiration

CHOOSE A TOTEM, YOUR VISUAL INSPIRATION

I AM WHAT IS KNOWN AS VISUALLY HYPERSENSITIVE. My need for order and organization and my desire to be surrounded by beautiful, meaningful tokens of my life is a constant balancing act for me.

It became helpful to remove the clutter around me, and since that is my business, I am good at it! I have daily practiced what I preach on myself and my family. Here's what I am left with at the end of more than a year of purging, re-sorting, and evaluating my environment: I am surrounded by things that represent happy moments, bring me comfort, inspire me to be creative, or are useful in some practical way.

Don't think for a minute that I don't have "stuff." I DO!! And I still make purchases. I love clothes and shoes and books, and well, you get the idea. But I have found that stuff is less satisfying than it once was, and that the memories made from the experiences I have with friends and family bring me more joy than any cute pair of shoes ever has.

I *do* appreciate having physical representations of my goals for my life, though. One of the most significant is the tattoo of a hummingbird that I wear on my left shoulder.

I love hummingbirds. They are bold, sassy, energetic birds. It may have been my imagination, but from the first day after my ex-husband moved out, there seemed to be the same bird hovering near my parked car every day as I left home. It would hover as I drove away, and it would greet me upon my return.

I felt happy with this connection, and researched the meaning of the hummingbird in Native American culture. I love that they represent joy and the celebration of life, that they fiercely protect their babies, and they have boundless energy. I knew then that my first tattoo needed to be a hummingbird. It has served as the visual representation of what I hold dear.

Getting a tattoo is a personal choice and not right for everyone. But I have never regretted having this bird on my shoulder, encouraging me to find joy and to be happy. And, yes, hummingbirds hover daily in my trees and roses. They *are* a joyful, personal inspiration.

let life's poetry
DANCE AROUND YOU

WEEK 48

LET LIFE'S POETRY DANCE AROUND YOU

As my first year of growth and change came to an end, I found joy more often and much to appreciate in the details of daily life. I have learned to pause and notice little things, life's poetry, and the beauty around me. Lyrics, books, and poetry are the lifelines that I will always cherish.

If you do not have a favorite poet or philosopher, perhaps now is a good time to find one to call your own. I first read David Whyte's beautiful poetry about a year ago. He writes of ordinary emotions and life moments in an extraordinary way. His writings are relatable and deeply philosophical.

There is one piece that really speaks to my soul titled "The Faces at Braga." Perhaps the connection is made all the dearer because I listened to a recording of him reciting this poem. He relates it with such passion and emotion that I cannot help but feel moved.

In it he speaks of the wood-carver's hands, a concept and image that brought me comfort in the early stages of my grief, and now when I read it, I am reminded to trust in the future that I am building. I take great comfort in that knowing.

If only our own faces
would allow the invisible carver's hand
to bring the deep grain of love to the surface.

If only we knew,
as the carver knew, how the flaws
in the wood led his searching chisel to the very core,

we would smile too
and not need faces immobilized
by fear and the weight of things undone.

By David Whyte[10]

10 Printed with permission from Many Rivers Press, www.davidwhyte.com. David Whyte, from "The Faces at Braga," *Where Many Rivers Meet,* © 1990 Many Rivers Press, Langley, WA USA.

trust
THERE
will
BE
another
BREATH

WEEK 49

TRUST THERE WILL
BE ANOTHER BREATH

It takes a leap of faith to trust what I cannot see or plan. But I do it every day in a million little ways. My faith that a universal spirit exists within and around me is comforting.

All that is required is for me to trust, and to breathe. Slowing down long enough to pay attention only to my breathing gives me the pause I need. After this reset, I am open to finding the answers to what is troubling me, or I can find the creative inspiration I need. I do not know if this is God's hand at work, but I *do* know that I do not feel alone in these moments.

I have practiced yoga for a long time. Many classes begin with slow, deep breathing rituals. I remember well an instructor who would ask as I inhaled slowly, and then exhaled for what felt like an eternity, to "trust that there will be a next breath."

At first, I found this deep, pranayama breathing painful. When my lungs were empty, I felt an almost frantic desperation for my next breath. When I calm my mind enough to relax in the moment and then just as slowly refill my lungs, I feel empowered and sense a shift in my well-being.

I have taken this pranayama breathing into my daily life. When I sense doubt or impending anxiety, I pause to slow down my breathing and relish the sense of calm that comes to me. It has certainly made the logjams of life, such as driving in traffic, more tolerable.

Deep breathing is a tool that I can take with me anywhere and everywhere I go. It makes such a difference.

MY
fears
WORSE
than
MY
reality

WEEK 50

MY FEARS WORSE THAN MY REALITY

As I look back at how far I have come over the more than a year that has passed since I agreed to divorce proceedings and mediation, I now know that my fears of the unknown were much different than my reality.

I felt shame and feared looking foolish. Letting go takes courage. I have replaced shame with self-respect, appreciation, and joy.

I feared loss of a familiar family life. Family life looks different now, but it is alive and well. Staying connected is a lifelong journey. I am learning to enjoy the roller coaster that we are riding. I savor the happy moments and tackle challenges with a growth mindset and great expectations. And, when I falter—and believe me, I do—I forgive myself and try again.

I feared loneliness. I have discovered strength and resilience. I have learned to embrace my solitude and to use it for reflection and rejuvenation.

I feared that I would not fill the hole in my life. It turns out there is no hole at all. It was an opportunity to grow in a new direction. I have rediscovered my passion for art and discovered that I enjoy writing. And I am enjoying the people in my life.

YOUR heart EXPANDS when it's BROKEN

WEEK 51

YOUR HEART EXPANDS
WHEN IT'S BROKEN

I HAVE HEARD IT SAID, AND I WILL QUOTE VICTORIA ERICKSON, THAT "YOUR HEART EXPANDS WHEN IT'S BROKEN. THE STRETCHING CREATES ROOM FOR EVEN MORE LOVE." The day I realized that my marriage was truly ending, I could not imagine ever feeling happy again. Yet here I sit, feeling so much more than happiness.

I am content. I feel relaxed. I have patience when I don't have all the answers. I recover more quickly from setbacks. I am proud of my resilience and fortitude. And I am much more fully present in my life.

For me, there were two choices: to close myself off from everything and everyone, or to risk it all again by allowing my heart to feel and express love and kindness and joy. As tempting as it was to stay locked up in that tight little closed-off place, I discovered that I didn't fit there.

I know that I have much to offer the people around me, and I accept that they won't *all* want or need what I bring to the world. And that's okay. This is a new experience of love.

My heart has expanded, and I see the world differently. I am excited to see where my life will lead me, and am savoring each new day with my whole heart.

the first year
WAS THE HARDEST

THE FIRST YEAR WAS THE HARDEST

I CAN HONESTLY SAY THAT *THEY* WERE RIGHT! The first year *was* the hardest. I am no longer that broken woman who first set out to save her marriage. I learned that letting go of what no longer serves me makes room for what I need now.

My one-year anniversary as a single woman has passed. I am mostly calm, but there is a restlessness growing in me. I am ready for something more in my life. And I am proud of who I am becoming.

Like it or not, those painful obstacles were an opportunity for growth and change. And, probably the most significant change is in how I view myself.

Selling the family home and finding a place to carve out my new life in a direction that suits me took a leap of faith. The safety net of what was familiar is gone. I am both nervous and excited as I navigate the bumpy, beautiful life I am living.

I have an even greater appreciation for my clients' struggles as I, too, have let go of many treasures. Letting go of the stuff of life is akin to saying goodbye to the part of my life that I know won't return. This knowing is bittersweet. I had to let go to make space for what is to come next.

I am mindful, I am hopeful, and I am joyful. I have people in my life that I love and cherish. I have found work that makes me happy and makes a difference to others. I do not have all the answers. But I *do* have plans and dreams for my future.

I have but one life; "*mais un vie.*" The time to live it is now!

ABOUT THE AUTHOR

Jennifer L. Raphael is the sole proprietor of Less-Stress Organizing Solutions in San Diego, California, a company she founded in 2013. Jennifer's areas of expertise are chronic disorganization and ADHD. Jennifer has personal experience with ADHD and has spent many years learning strategies to cope with it and ways to encourage others with this neuro-atypical brain style.

She has been a blogger since March 2012, when she began sharing personal anecdotes about her own challenges with disorganization. This blossomed into a blog featuring helpful strategies regarding residential organizing and personal productivity.

Jennifer is an RN, BSN, and a member of CHADD (Children and Adults with ADHD), ICD (Institute for Challenging Disorganization), and NAPO (National Association of Productivity and Organizing Professionals).

Jennifer lives with her daughter, Brenna, her cats Gabby and Gandalf the Grey, and her dog, Parker. When she isn't working or at home, she can be found at the beach, the theater, or hanging out with friends.

ACKNOWLEDGMENTS

To my daughter, Brenna, I couldn't be more grateful for your love and support. Not once have you questioned my need to write this book or expressed concern about its contents. Your unconditional love and faith in me is such a blessing. A special note of thanks for the beautiful painting that graces the book cover. You have an extraordinary talent.

To my son, Trevor, I am grateful for your capacity to forgive and to stay true to yourself.

Thank you to my friends Chris Slaven and Tandy DeLisle. You have listened endlessly to my story and still call me a friend after seeing my darkest side. I am so grateful for your friendships.

To the friends who have shown compassion, humor, and what solidarity amongst women means: Rhonda, Cheri, Suzanne, and Jackie—you rock!

To my sage advisors and colleagues at Hera Hub San Diego, Melody, Laurie, and Sarah, thank you for inspiring me.

To my therapist, Kenneth Buhr, PhD. I am forever grateful for your wise counsel and your capacity for kindness. Not once have I felt judged in your presence.

To my parents and family for always loving me, even when I was at my moodiest. I love you.

When I first began writing this book, Bethany Kelly, my Publishing Partner, told me, "You will be a different person when you finish this book." Thank you, Bethany, for encouraging me every step along the way and for believing my story is worth telling. You have become my friend through this process.

To my copy editor, Frank Steele, and design editor, Stefan Merour, I could not have finished this book without your support and expertise. Thank you both for your dedication to excellence.

And, finally, to my ex-husband. Thank you for the opportunity to learn I can find light in the darkness. I hope you find what you are seeking.